AFRICAN CRAFTS
FOR YOU TO MAKE

by Janet and Alex D'Amato

Julian Messner   New York

Contents

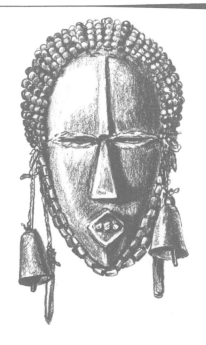

Published simultaneously in the United States and Canada by Julian Messner, a division of Simon & Schuster, Inc., 1 West 39th Street, New York, N. Y. 10018. All rights reserved.

Copyright, ©, 1969 by Janet and Alex D'Amato

Fifth Printing, 1975

Printed in the United States of America
ISBNO-671-32129-3-TRADE CLOTH
ISBNO-671-32130-7-MCE
Library of Congress Catalog Card No. 70-75690

Introduction

The tribes of Africa are centuries old, and over the years they have contributed great pieces of art and intricate crafts. This book describes some of the crafts made in Africa south of the Sahara. The farms of West Africa, tropical forests of the Congo, southern grasslands, and eastern plains have each contributed different types of crafts. Shown are examples from various areas—some from ancient kingdoms, others more recent. Farming tribes generally made more objects and had more rituals than nomadic, or wandering, tribes. To find any tribe mentioned, check the map.

Most of the examples of African crafts in this book are made of wood. Most wooden objects found in Africa today are not more than 150 years old, as wood decays rapidly in a hot, damp climate. But the styles of these examples developed from traditions that were passed on for centuries.

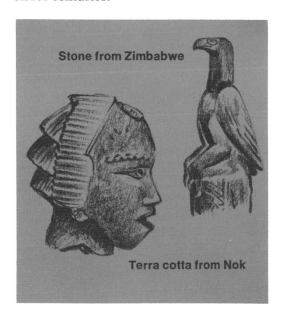

Stone from Zimbabwe

Terra cotta from Nok

Stone carvings and ancient clay figures have been found. The most ancient, small heads from Nok, were believed to have been made as far back as 1000 B.C.

The ancient Africans made more use of metal than most primitive peoples. (The term *primitive* as used here does not mean untrained or untalented. The craftsman was often very highly regarded and was an important member of the community. The term *primitive* is generally applied to areas where there was no written language.) Iron tools have been used in Africa for many centuries, and other metals such as gold, silver, and bronze were shaped into statues and decorations as far back as the 13th century, possibly earlier.

Beadwork was used for personal adornment. Some tribes covered whole masks, thrones, and statues with beads. Other crafts included ivory carving, wicker work, fine fiber weaving, and pottery.

Crafts were extremely vital in ancient Africa, for people depended upon them to pass on their heritage. Techniques were passed on from one generation to the next. Sculpture replaced the written word. Abstractions and symbols were not mere decoration used at the whim of the artist, but an established language understood by the tribe. Distortion was used to stress importance.

Religion touched everything in daily life. Generally there was a belief in a creator who was too great to be contained in symbols or statues, as well as a belief in many lesser gods, demons, and spirits. The ancient Africans believed that living spirits dwelled in all things—plants, animals, and

Introduction continued

man. This belief was expressed in all of their work. The spirit of the tree, for example, had to be pleased to obtain a good sculpture from its wood. Spirits of those who had died were believed to wander about the village until ancestor figures were carved to house them.

Masks and costumes hid the identity of the wearer so he *became* the spirit he represented. No one lied to a spirit. Disputes were settled and moral codes enforced by masked figures. The masked figures can be appreciated best when seen in motion. After you make mask, create a dance and perform it in a dim light to drum beats. In some areas, body paint was used instead of masks.

Practically all art was religious. In some early kingdoms, however, sculpture glorified the king, showing his wealth and powers. Elaborate wall panels of bronze, thrones, and scepters were among the objects created for the court. Household items were intended primarily for practical use. Any decoration on such objects probably originated for a ritual purpose.

Face from a Picasso Painting

Basonge Mask

If possible, look at examples of ancient African art in a museum. This book will give instructions for constructing copies of various African objects. By actually going through the process of creating such objects yourself, you can better appreciate them. The proportion, exaggeration, and contrasts in texture will become more apparent to you as you work. Try to understand the emotional involvement felt by the craftsman of the original object, although this is difficult as you do not share his beliefs.

Read the instructions completely through before you start. Gather your materials. After you make some of the items described here, you may want to create your own. In the early part of this century, great European artists such as Picasso and Klee studied African art and used it as inspiration for their creations. This book should give you many ideas and techniques to get you started with crafts, as well as help you understand African crafts and the African heritage.

Bronze Wall Panel from Benin

General Instructions and Materials:

The materials you will need will depend upon which projects you choose to do. Scissors, pencils, paper, an awl, and a knife will generally be needed. It might be a good idea to start a box of odds and ends: things like string, broken necklaces, jewelry, empty plastic bottles, egg cartons, pipe cleaners, feathers, gift-wrap cords, and sewing trims.

Other materials you may need include styrofoam, available in craft shops and sometimes in dime stores; it can be cut out with a coping saw or knife. Raffia and reeds, also available in craft stores, should be worked wet. White glue is best when working with wood. Household cement holds best on surfaces that are shiny or dissimilar. Masking tape is available in craft, art, and hardware stores. Transparent tape should be used where you do not want the tape to show. Wire of various kinds is available in hardware stores. For small pieces of wire, straighten a paper clip and cut size needed.

Craft and dime stores carry many types of beads. Seed beads are tiny and need a special needle for stringing. Tubettini, a type of macaroni, is available in all supermarkets. To color, soak in vegetable dye. Make larger beads of clay or use old jewelry.

Paints:

In Africa, until recently, colors were made of available natural materials, basically white, black and red. White, made of clay or lime was called kaolin and symbolized death and unknown forces. Black was obtained from soot. Red was made from the Camwood tree. When ground up and mixed with certain oils from tree bark, it made a red paint called tukula. Besides having magical properties, this red paint also protected the carving from termites.

On your crafts, you can paint large areas with latex household paint. Smaller areas can be colored with water-color paints. A drop of white glue added to a small dish of water color will help make the paint waterproof if you wish to antique over it. When finished, be sure to wash the brush before it dries.

Most carvings were made of wood, darkened. To reproduce such a finish, use a regular wood stain from the hardware store or use brown liquid shoe polish. Darken with a second coat of black paste polish. Polish with a cloth to give the object an appearance of having grown beautiful with age. Other wood colors were enhanced by burying the object in mud or rubbing in ashes and soot. You can achieve this affect by coating over a painted object with wood stain and rubbing it off. An old weathered look will make the things you create look more authentic.

For metallic finishes, use a small can of spray paint purchased at dime, hobby, or craft stores. Spray the object, preferably outdoors, in a box with papers behind it. Gold finishes that can be rubbed on are also available in tubes at craft and hardware stores. Use sparingly for best effect.

Materials continued

Clay:

Unless otherwise specified, clay should be the kind that dries hard when exposed to air. It is available in many forms in toy, craft, and dime stores. For a homemade version, here is a recipe:

Mix together 1 cup salt, 1 cup baking soda, 1 cup corn starch. Add 1⅓ cups of cold water. Mix until all dry ingredients are completely dissolved. Cook over medium heat, stirring until very thick. Cool, knead. Mix in food coloring for tints. Keep clay in a plastic bag until needed. When working, wet fingers to smooth surface. When clay is dry and hard, it can be painted.

Patterns:

In most cases, squared areas for patterns are given. Where they are not, work from an illustration of the object. Lay a piece of lightweight tracing paper over the picture. Trace off outline. Draw squares ½ʺ apart over this (Fig. 1). To enlarge, take a larger sheet of paper, draw the same number of squares on it, but larger, as directed for that object. For example ½ʺ becomes 1ʺ, which doubles the size. Make a heavier middle line on both squared sheets as a guide. Working out from center, draw the outline of the object on the larger squares, counting corre-

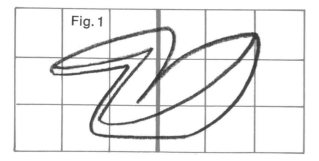

Fig. 1

sponding squares (Fig. 2), and drawing the same lines as in the smaller squares. This makes it easy to get proper proportions on an enlarged shape.

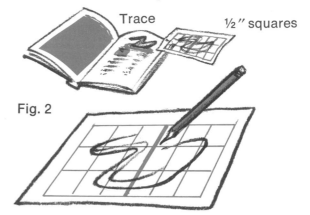

Trace   ½ʺ squares

Fig. 2

Large Pattern to work from 1ʺ squares

Papier-Mache:

There are several kinds of papier-mâché. For objects of a larger size, you will need an armature or form to work on. This armature can be made of bottles taped together, wire, styrofoam, anything for a basic inside shape. For some projects you will be given specific instruction for making the armature.

There is a short-cut method of making papier-mâché over an armature. Tear 1ʺ strips of newspaper and soak in a solution of 1 cup of water and ¼ cup of wallpaper paste. Pull one strip at a time between fingers to remove excess paste (Fig. 1). Lay strips around form, crossing strips at various angles. This holds the shape together and begins to build up contours (Fig. 2). Crumpled pieces of newspaper can be added between layers for thickness. Strips of paper toweling or tissue, soaked in paste, make a final layer.

For a better finish, use true papier-mâché. To make, tear newsprint into pieces about ¼" square. Soak in water several days until mushy. Squeeze and knead into a pulp. Squeeze out excess water. Gradually add wallpaper paste to the pulp. The mixture should be thick but not too sticky, about the consistency of soft modeling clay. Knead and shape your models. As it dries, wet hands to smooth final surfaces (Fig. 3).

There are packages of prepared papier-mâché available in craft stores; all you add is water. Some brands, such as Celluclay, sculpture beautifully.

Allow several days drying time, depending on the thickness of the object. Throughout the book, we have suggested various combinations of these methods.

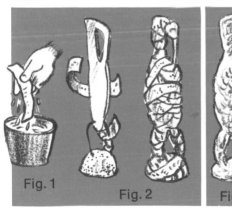

Fig. 1   Fig. 2   Fig. 3

Woodcarving:

Wood carving should be done with a sharp pocket knife or craft knife. Other wood-carving tools are helpful but not necessary.

Balsa wood is the easiest to work. Pieces of all sizes and thicknesses are available in art and craft stores.

After drawing the front view of a pattern on the wood block, cut away excess with a coping saw or vibrating jig saw (Fig. 1). Turn, draw in shape for side view. Trim off any excess areas from this view (Fig. 2). Then whittle carefully, cutting small pieces at a time. Turn piece constantly to see how overall shape is progressing. To cut small wedge-shaped pieces, cut at angle as shown (Fig. 3).

Always keep your finger behind the knife and cut away from you. It might be advisable to first practice on a scrap piece. You will find balsa wood easy to whittle once you have practiced.

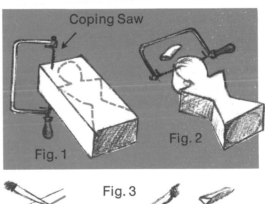

Coping Saw

Fig. 1   Fig. 2

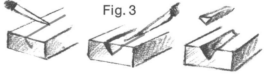

Fig. 3

Dowels, which are round wooden sticks, can be purchased in all diameters in craft and hardware stores and lumber yards.

If you prefer papier-mâché to wood, many wood projects can be adapted, using the patterns given. Or vice-versa, papier-mâché objects can be carved in wood, but you may need larger pieces of wood and extra carving tools.

Ashanti Doll (Akua-ba)

Women of the Ashanti tribe carried a decorative doll tucked into their waistbands. They believed it would make their unborn children beautiful and well-formed. The doll shown here has a round head, but some were fashioned with square heads.

The people of the Yoruba tribe believed that if one of a pair of twin babies died, a doll had to be cared for just as the living twin would have been, and carried by the mother. This Yoruba doll (Ibeji) was carved in a somewhat realistic style.

Shape and carve balsa wood to the dimensions shown for the body. It should be 1″ thick at the base, tapering up to ¾″ in diameter at the neck (Fig. 1). Carve indentations around neck (Fig. 2) to form three neck rings.

The base is 2″ in diameter, 1″ high. To prevent the doll from tipping too easily, carve a hole in the bottom and insert a fishing or drapery weight (Fig. 3). Fill in hole around weight with plastic wood.

To make arms, cut ½″ thick wood and taper out to a point at end (Fig. 4). The head is a 5″ circle of ¼″ thick wood. Carve or use a wood-burning tool to make designs on back of head (Fig. 5).

BODY

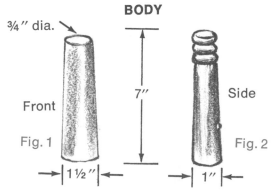

¾″ dia.

7″

Front

Fig. 1

1½″

Side

Fig. 2

1″

To get shape and placement of features, enlarge face pattern. Cut eyebrows, nose, mouth out of ¼″ wood, then shape. Triangular-shaped eyes should be about 3/16″ thick. Glue features in place.

To assemble doll, straighten a paper clip and cut 1″ pieces. Push these into wood of base, arms, and neck as shown (Fig. 6). Add glue and push on head, arms, and base. Paint completed doll brown with shoe polish.

Soak tubettini (a type of macaroni) in yellow food coloring. When dry, make an 18″ string of the macaroni and loosely wrap it three times above base. Tie (Fig. 7). String a necklace of old beads of various sizes and colors about 5½″ long. Tie at neck.

For earrings, thread a needle and tie a knot in thread. Push needle through hole from behind where indicated (Fig. 8). String 2″ of seed beads of various colors, return needle through the same hole, knot and glue thread behind.

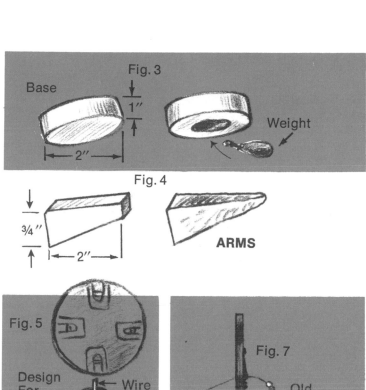

Fig. 3

Base

1″

2″

Weight

Fig. 4

¾″

2″

ARMS

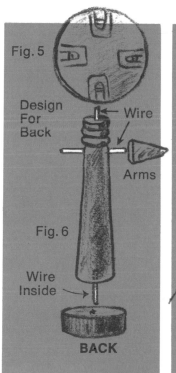

Fig. 5

Design For Back

Wire

Arms

Fig. 6

Wire Inside

BACK

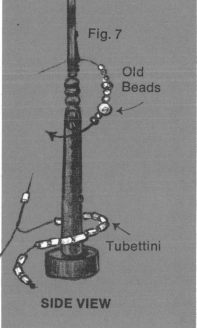

Fig. 7

Old Beads

Tubettini

SIDE VIEW

FACE PATTERN   ½″ = 1″

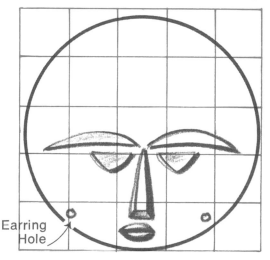

Earring Hole

Fig. 8

Beads

Barotse Bowl

The best known crafts of the Barotse tribe of Zambia were carved oval bowls and other wooden items for practical household use. The tops of these bowls were expertly fitted and the figures on top were somewhat geometric.

Make your bowl by starting with a shallow round plastic bowl about 6″ across. For a cover, trace the top of the bowl on cardboard and cut out a circle that is ½″ wider all around (Fig. 1). To make cover fit inside of bowl, cut two circular pieces of cardboard ½″ less than the diameter of the top of the bowl (Fig. 2). Glue or tape together (Fig. 3). To make cover look like carved wood, add a layer of papier-mâché about ½″ thick on top. Use a very thin layer of papier-mâché on underside of cover to make sure it fits. Shape about a ¼″ layer around outside of bowl (Fig. 4).

Enlarge bird shape above to proper size to fit your cover. Carve two birds out of balsa wood. Glue birds to cover. When dry, paint bowl, cover, and birds a rich dark-brown and varnish or wax polish to give them a shine.

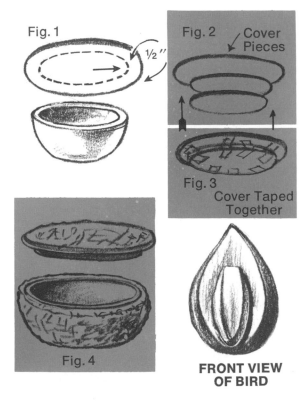

Fig. 1

Fig. 2 Cover Pieces

½″

Fig. 3 Cover Taped Together

Fig. 4

FRONT VIEW OF BIRD

Tie-Die Fabrics

Fabrics were woven on many different types of looms. The Yoruba and other tribes sometimes made a fabric with a deep plush effect. Some tribes made designs by sewing small pieces of fabric to the cloth. We call this appliqué. Cloth from many areas had the pattern woven in. The Ashanti and Mangbetu were among the tribes that painted or stamped patterns onto the fabric.

Yoruba and other tribes used various "resist" methods to obtain patterns. They would prevent the dye from taking in certain planned areas by applying wax or other materials. After dying, the wax was removed and these areas remained their original color.

In the Cameroons and Nigeria and among the people of the Baulé tribe, the fabric was folded and tied around seeds, stones, and sticks before being dyed, usually with indigo. This method created interesting patterns.

For an example of the last method, cut a piece of white fabric about 8″ square (a piece of an old sheet is fine). Cut a 1″ diameter dowel about 6″ long, or use a wooden handle or straight clothespin or any unpainted wooden stick. Lay fabric over stick. Tie a string around top (Fig. 1). Adjust fabric so gathers are fairly even all around, with no big folds (Fig. 2). Take another piece of string and tie below several times (Fig. 3).

For dye, mix about ¼ cup of blue vegetable dye (food coloring). Make it quite strong. Dip and dab tied pieces so the exposed areas are colored. Leave tip white. Press out excess dye with a rag and allow to dry.

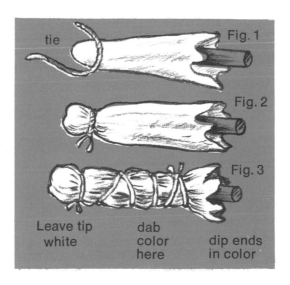

tie — Fig. 1
Fig. 2
Fig. 3
Leave tip white — dab color here — dip ends in color

When dry, cut off string and open up fabric to discover what design you have created! Press flat.

The way you fold the fabric and tie the string and where you put the color creates the pattern. To get different designs, try tying and dying several pieces.

Bambara Spoon

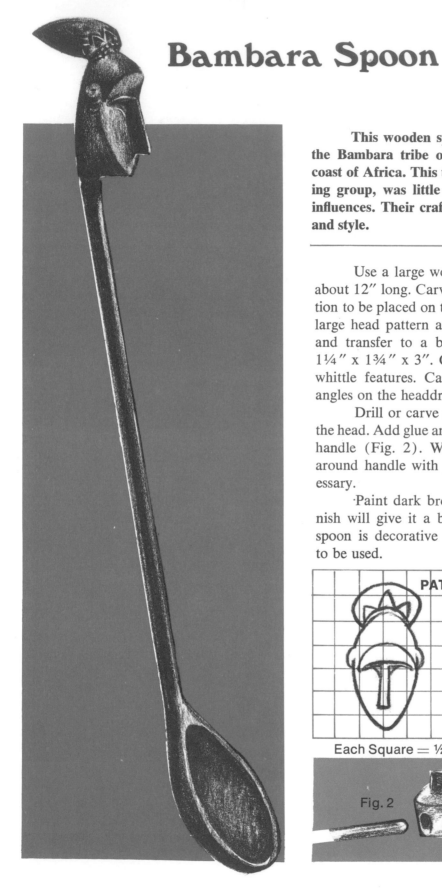

This wooden spoon was carved by the Bambara tribe of Mali on the west coast of Africa. This tribe, a settled farming group, was little affected by outside influences. Their crafts show much grace and style.

Use a large wooden mixing spoon, about 12″ long. Carve a head for decoration to be placed on top of the spoon. Enlarge head pattern as indicated (Fig. 1) and transfer to a block of balsa wood 1¼″ x 1¾″ x 3″. Cut away excess and whittle features. Carve in the little triangles on the headdress.

Drill or carve a hole at the base of the head. Add glue and insert end of spoon handle (Fig. 2). When glue is dry, fill around handle with plastic wood if necessary.

·Paint dark brown. A layer of varnish will give it a better finish, but this spoon is decorative now and not meant to be used.

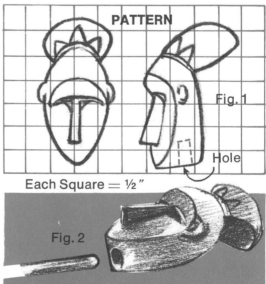

PATTERN

Fig. 1

Hole

Each Square = ½″

Fig. 2

Mankala (a game)

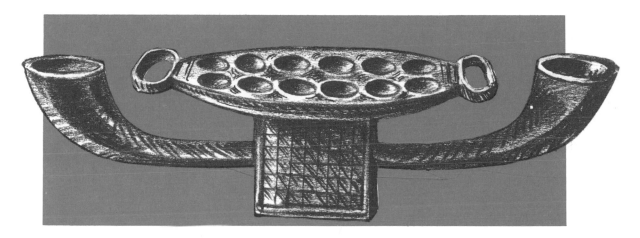

Mankala is a game believed to have originated in Asia Minor. Through the centuries it has been played all over Africa with many variations.

This board is an example from Sierra Leone. In some tribes, only the king could play, and his board was beautifully carved and decorated. Often the whole tribe watched. Most boards were for two players, but some versions were made for many players. When a caravan stopped to rest, people would scoop out twelve holes in the sand and play. Small boys would also make a board this way.

Playing pieces, or Hasa, were shells, smooth rocks, or nuts.

You can make a very simple version of the beautifully carved game board shown above. On the following pages are rules so you can play this game with a friend.

To make your game board, use a 12″ molded egg carton. Cut off top (use later for base). Cut off tips of points projecting in the middle between cups. Fold in so middle section is level (Fig. 1).

For base, use a board about 16″ long, 3″ wide, ½″ thick. Sand smooth, and round the corners slightly. Thumb tack and glue cover of egg carton in the center of this board (Fig. 2).

Cut down two paper cups, making them about 2″ high. Tack and glue the cups to the board on either end. Put bottom half (with the egg cups) of carton into the inverted cover on the base and tape together. Use papier-mâché to cover holes of middle section. Add a thin layer of papier-mâché to sides and ends (Fig. 3). When dry, paint light tan.

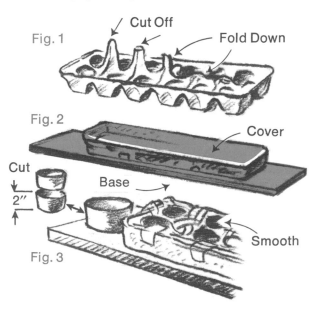

Fig. 1 — Cut Off — Fold Down

Fig. 2 — Cover — Base

Cut 2″ — Base — Smooth

Fig. 3

Mankala – Rules of the Game

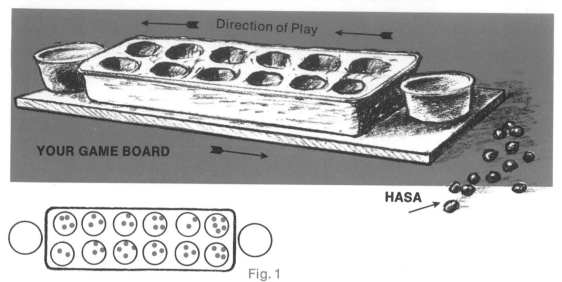

Direction of Play

YOUR GAME BOARD

HASA

Fig. 1

Rules for a game for two players:

This is a simplified version of one of the ways Mankala was played. You will need about forty playing pieces, or Hasa as they were called in some areas. For your Hasa you can use buttons, beads, or small marbles. They should all be about the same size and shape (¼″ to ½″ around).

One player, let's call him B, sets up the board, putting no less than two or no more than five Hasa in each of the twelve holes. Use up all forty Hasa (Fig. 1). The number of Hasa in each hole can be varied with each game.

All the diagrams are an example of one play. The number of Hasa will vary with each play in each game.

The other player (player A) starts from the hole indicated (Fig. 2). He picks up all the Hasa in this hole and, starting with the next hole to the right, drops one Hasa at a time into each successive hole.

Fig. 2

Example of play when starting hole contained 4 Hasa

Player **A**
Starting Hole

A Cup

B Cup

Drop one Hasa in Each Hole

Last Hole

Player **B** Starting Hole

Direction of Move

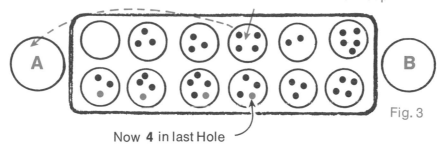

A wins Hasa in Opposite Hole,
Transfers Hasa to **A** cup

Fig. 3

Now **4** in last Hole

When he drops his last one in, he checks the number of Hasa in this last hole. If it now contains *two* or *four* Hasa, this player takes all the Hasa in the hole on the opposite side of the game board (Fig. 3).

Player A removes the Hasa from the opposite hole, as indicated, and puts them in his cup in front of him. These are the Hasa he has won.

Then player A continues playing around the game board by returning to the last hole into which he originally dropped the last Hasa. He picks up all the Hasa in this hole and continues around the board, dropping one in each hole until he gets to the last hole (Fig. 4). Then he checks again to see how many Hasa are in this

last hole. If there are two or four, again he wins the Hasa in the opposite hole. He continues playing until he drops his last Hasa into an *empty* hole. When this happens, it is the end of his turn. The other player (B) starts from his starting hole and continues around with the same procedure. The Hasa he wins he places in B's cup.

On each turn, begin at the starting hole unless it is empty. In this case, begin at the first hole to the right that does contain Hasa, picking up and dropping in each hole as before.

When too few Hasa remain to be able to win any more, the game is finished. Each player counts up the Hasa in his cup, and the one with the most wins.

Fig. 4

In this case, only 3 Hasa in last hole so **A** cannot win Hasa from Opposite hole. **A** picks up these 3 and continues

A continues Play

Pick up four Hasa from "Last" hole, drops them in successive holes

Money

The African medium of exchange, or money, has ranged through the centuries from blocks of salt to cubes of gold. The barter system served most areas in early times, but some kingdoms developed various forms of currency.

Iron was used to make many money objects including heavy spear shapes up to four feet long. Ivory was used in its natural state or carved into shapes. Copper and various alloys were shaped into many forms, from ingots (bars) to anklets. Gold dust (see next page) and gold objects were important mediums of exchange. The most universally used form of money was the cowry shell. It had established value and was supposed to have magical powers. Strung together, cowry shells were often used for decoration. Some costumes and masks had the surfaces nearly covered with these shells.

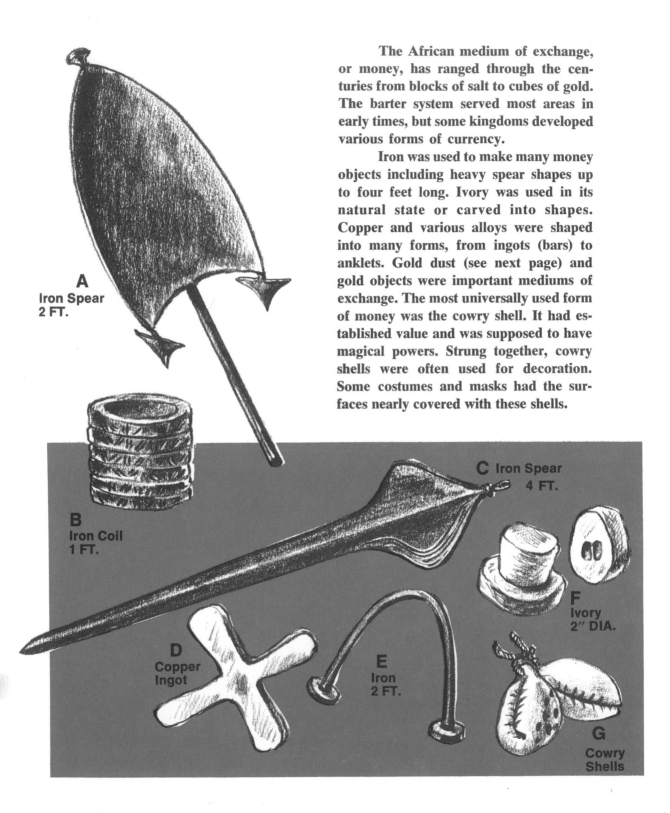

A
Iron Spear
2 FT.

B
Iron Coil
1 FT.

C Iron Spear
4 FT.

D
Copper
Ingot

E
Iron
2 FT.

F
Ivory
2″ DIA.

G
Cowry
Shells

To make an exhibit of models of some of the currency of Africa, here are some suggestions.

To make *A*, use aluminum sheeting or the side from a soft-drink can. Remove ends from soft drink can, cut down the seam, and flatten. Enlarge pattern of shape *A*. Cut out of the aluminum two identical shapes. Cut a flat stick or thin dowel 12″ long. Glue the two metal shapes together with the stick between (Fig. 1). Use clip clothespins to hold edges while drying. For top knob, leave about ¼″ of stick protruding above metal. Wrap this ¼″ piece with aluminum foil to shape knob (Fig. 2). Twist the triangular points so they are at a 90° angle to the flat area of the spear shape.

To make *B*, use a self-hardening clay, roll out, and cut into strips. Coil around and flatten to look like the drawing. Make designs on the surface with a pointed tool (Fig. 3). Allow to dry.

Shapes *C* and *D* should be cast in a nonhardening clay mold (described on page 63). Make patterns from drawings so that ½″ = 1″. Indent clay mold so that the form is about ½″ deep (Fig. 4). Cut a thin cardboard piece slightly smaller than shape *C*. Put a layer of plaster in mold, lay on shape, add more plaster to fill mold. When plaster is slightly dry, scratch decoration lines along one side of *C*.

Shape *E* could be made of wire or pipe cleaners, with buttons taped and glued to ends.

To make *F*, use a hardening type of clay. Roll out and make shapes shown about 2″ around. When dry, paint yellowish-white to look like ivory. Finish with a coat of clear nail polish.

For *G*, glue a piece of string inside each of two shells. Tie together. If you don't have real cowry shells, shape them from clay and finish the same way as *F*. Paint on brown dots to look like shell design (Fig. 5).

When shapes are thoroughly dry, spray shapes *A*, *B*, *C*, *E* black. Spray *D* copper.

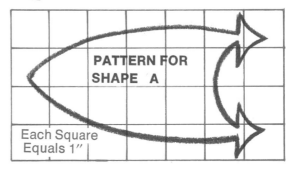

PATTERN FOR SHAPE A

Each Square Equals 1″

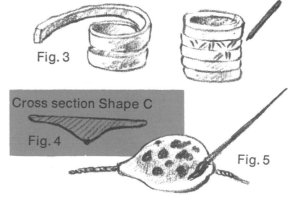

Fig. 1

Knob

Fig. 2 ← Twist

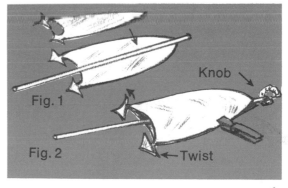

Fig. 3

Cross section Shape C

Fig. 4

Fig. 5

Gold Weights

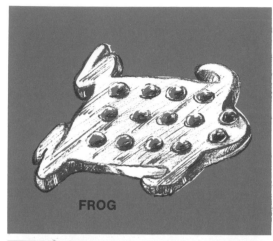

FROG

PORCUPINE

SNAKE

Before the invention of coins or before European currency reached Africa about three hundred years ago, gold dust was used as money by the Baulé and Ashanti tribes. To trade, a man had to carry his own scales, gold dust, and graduated weights with him. A weight on one side of the scales balanced the proper amount of gold dust on the other.

These weights were cast of bronze or brass by a complex method called Cire Perdue, or Lost Wax. Tiny figures, usually about three inches long, were shaped in wax, then surrounded by soft clay. When dry and hardened, the clay formed the mold. The mold was heated, and the wax evaporated. Then it was filled with molten bronze. When the bronze cooled, the clay was broken away and the bronze figure was exactly the same shape as the original wax one.

The weights had many forms: Geometric shapes, animals, plants, and people illustrated myths, customs, and everyday life. The king and the wealthy classes had great collections, enjoying them for their shapes and using them as charms and ornaments, as well as for their original purpose.

Large bronzes in Ife and Benin were made by a process similiar to Lost Wax. The wax was shaped in a thin layer over a solid core. Then the clay mold was made around it, the wax burned off, and the metal poured in. When the clay was broken away, supports and air vents had to be carefully filed off and the intricate pieces smoothed and finished.

Using the drawings as guides, shape desired creature in clay 3″ to 4″ long. Use a knife or pointed stick to poke and shape. For chameleon, unfold a paper clip and mold clay shape around it (Fig. 1). If a piece breaks, it can be glued back together when clay is dry. For snake, use a roll of clay and coil it around. When dry, glue on beads for eyes. Cut frog of ¼″ thick layer of clay, add textures, shape legs.

Add the chameleon's swirled spots after the clay is dry. Cut 1½″ pieces of soft fine string. Dilute a small amount of white glue with water. Soak string, then wind a flat spiral, and stick on (Fig. 2). Add a little dab of the thinned glue to help it adhere. Continue over figure as shown (Fig. 3). Keep a wet towel handy to clean tools and fingers as they get sticky.

When the clay porcupine is dry, cut pieces of fine string or button-hole thread 2″ to 3″ long. Soak as above. Stick on back, leaving ends sticking out. Lay a few on, let dry, add another layer. Continue until the figure looks like a porcupine.

In making all of the figures, wait several days to be sure glue and clay are thoroughly dry, then spray gold.

GOAT

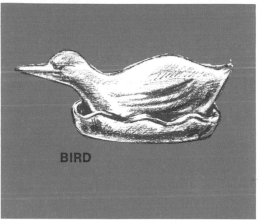

BIRD

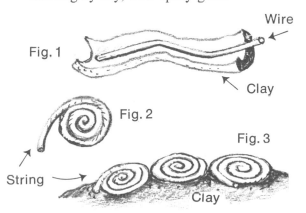

Fig. 1

Wire

Clay

Fig. 2

String

Fig. 3

Clay

CHAMELEON

N'Debele House

In most parts of Africa, houses were round with conical straw tops. The wall materials varied according to what materials were accessible. Some had no side walls. Instead, sticks were set in the ground in a circle, curved, and tied up at the top center.

Sometimes the roof, of a larger diameter than side walls, was supported on separate poles. This gave a porch effect all around for shade. Some areas had square houses with peaked roofs of straw. Many tribes painted the walls with designs. Others lined interior walls with woven mats.

The homes of the N'Debele were decorated with great pride. The new bride painted gay designs on the walls she had made surrounding the house. She renewed these after rains. Furniture was practically nonexistent. People sat on raised clay platforms and slept on woven mats. The N'Debele woman kept her house clean with a gaily beaded broom.

For base of house and courtyard, use a board 14″ x 16″ and cover with a thin layer of tan clay. Mark out floor plan (Fig. 1). Roll out tan clay ½″ thick. For courtyard walls, measure 1″ to 2″ wide and long enough to fit areas. See Fig. 2 for outlines to follow. Cut walls. Leave openings for gates. Place ⅜″ clay slabs in position for seats (see floor plan). Poke a hole in backyard where tree will be inserted. Lay walls flat. Let walls and base dry separately.

Meanwhile, make the house. Use a coffee can or similar size can or round box. Roll clay out about ⅜″ thick. Wrap around can, but cut out space for door. When partially dry, put a rubber band around top to hold clay in place. Position house on base and blend in clay around bottom.

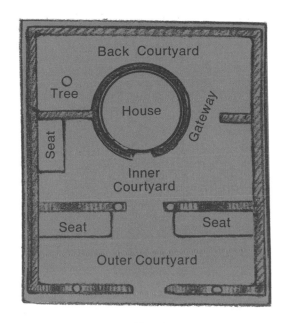

Fig. 1

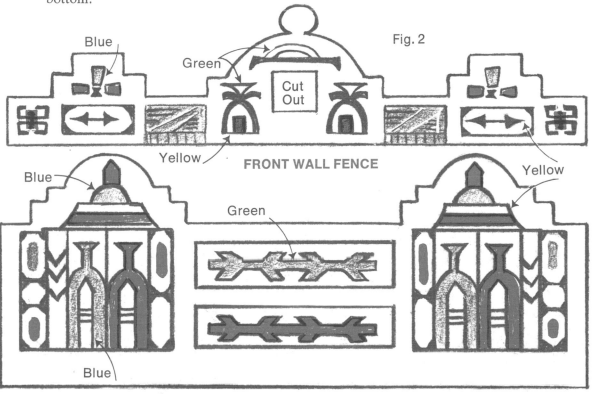

Fig. 2

FRONT WALL FENCE

INNER COURTYARD WALL FENCE

N'Debele House continued

For roof, cut a cardboard circle ½″ larger than the diameter of the can. Use six or eight 8″ plastic soda straws. Fold straws in half, tie at center. Spread out and staple ends to the cardboard circle you have cut (Fig. 4). Loop a string around about halfway between cardboard and peak. Tie. Cut strips of raffia or tan crepe paper about 6″ long (Fig. 5). Tie at one end and place this at top peak. Tie in place. Spread out evenly and sew with raffia to the straw frame at midpoint (Fig. 5). For top layer, add another bunch of raffia about 3″ long (Fig. 6). Tie to top and trim ends even. Wind a piece of raffia around top knob to hide ends and glue to hold (Fig. 7). Glue finished roof to top of house.

When walls are thoroughly dry, paint front of walls white, then paint on black outlines of designs (Fig. 2). Fill in with blue, green, yellow, and brownish-red as indicated.

Fig. 3   **PATTERN SIDE WALLS**

Paint side walls gray, then paint on black and white fence designs (Fig. 3).

Glue walls in position on base, adding extra clay and blending it around wall bases to hold. Glue a piece of wood-grained paper in door opening of the house. For tree, add a twig with bits of green sponge glued on.

These houses and courtyards were built next to each other. The side walls of one courtyard were used for the side of the neighbor's yard. Build a village if you like, varying wall shapes and designs.

ROOF

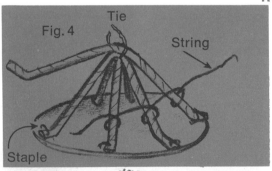

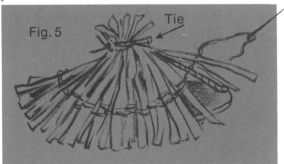

Kano House

Most of the people of Kano, a city in Nigeria, are followers of the religion of Islam. Since ancient times, Kano, like Timbukto and Niamey, other cities that also bordered on the Sahara Desert, was a crossroads for camel caravans. In cities such as these the houses wcrc usually square, sometimes round, made of reddish-brown mud. Walls enclosed a courtyard; windows were small to keep out the heat.

Construct this house using a box about 6″ x 4″ x 4″. The base should be about 9″ x 14″. Cover with thin layer of brown clay.

Cut a door and window out of box (see illustration). Poke 1½″ sticks in corners .

Roll out brown clay about ¼″ thick. Cover box and make shapes on corners around the sticks as shown (Fig. 1). For rain spouts, cut soda straws 1″ long, slice in half (Fig. 2). Poke into clay where shown. Make fence walls of clay ½″ thick and 4″ high as shown. Add spouts to wall. Seat is a piece of clay ¾″ thick. Paint black and white designs on front.

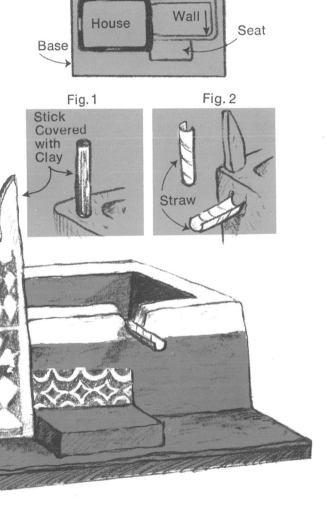

Floor Plan

Base — House — Wall — Seat

Fig. 1
Stick Covered with Clay

Fig. 2
Straw

Chad House

These houses, built around Lake Chad, were made of woven rushes and mud. The people were farmers and fishermen.

One of the better crafts of this area was leather work. The leather was often dyed a reddish hue and designs were cut into it or painted or embroidered on. Small strips were plaited or many pieces sewn together like patchwork. Sometimes small contrasting pieces were sewn on to a larger piece of leather.

For the base of house use a ½″ thick piece of styrofoam covered with a thin layer of brown clay. Construct house around a coffee can or salt box as described on page 22. Instead of covering with clay, glue on woven straw from an old beach hat or bag (Fig. 1), or use a coarsely-woven fabric like monks cloth. Paint door black.

To make fence, poke 3″ sticks into the styrofoam base. To hold up fence, wind a wire or pipe cleaner around top of one stick and over to the next stick (Fig. 2). Cut strips of the woven straw or fabric 2½″ high. Lace with raffia or twine into straw, up over wire and down, to hold up fence (Fig. 3).

To add realism, make clay pots ½″ to 2″ high, and pile bunches of firewood (little sticks) around yard.

These villages were clusters of many houses, each with their own fences. Make several houses for a village.

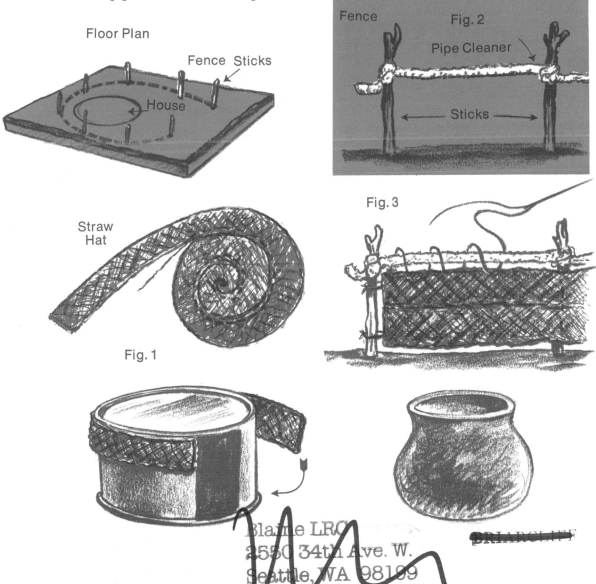

Floor Plan

Fence Sticks

House

Fence   Fig. 2

Pipe Cleaner

← Sticks →

Fig. 3

Straw Hat

Fig. 1

Nuba House of Sudan

This grouping of huts housed a family. The front hut was a gateway. Each parent had his own hut. The children had a hut, where grain was stored also. Often there were five or six huts in the circle depending on the number of children. Guests slept in the gateway hut.

The round doors in the other huts were raised to keep out rodents. Domestic animals were kept in the courtyard. An ostrich egg sometimes decorated the peak of the huts.

Make these houses by following the instructions on page 21. Use a round salt box for the base of each house. Cut down to 3″ high. Cut in round doors except for gatehouse. Add a round clay knob on top of each roof. Make curved clay walls. Set houses on a clay covered base. Put plastic domestic animals in courtyard.

Kikuyu House of Kenya

These houses had exceptionally high pointed roofs. The walls were made of mud. Make this similar to the hut on page 21 except for the roof. Cut twelve straws 7″ long, gather and tie at one end. Staple other ends to the cardboard circle. Cover as before, cutting raffia 8″ long for bottom layer and 3″ for top layer. Add a round clay base and paint door black.

Basonge Bell

Africans made bells in a great variety of shapes and materials. In the ancient kingdom of Benin, bells were cast in bronze and ornately decorated with heads or animal figures, such as the sacred mudfish.

Other tribes, such as the Watusi, tied bells similar to our jingle bells to their ankles during dances. In many areas people made crude metal bells for their cattle or dogs.

This wooden bell was made by the Basonge tribe of the Congo.

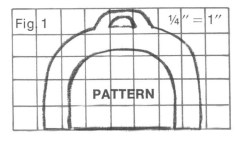

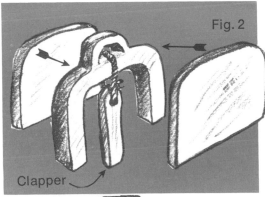

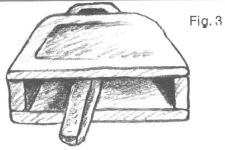

Enlarge pattern to 5″ x 6″. Cut this shape with a coping saw or jig saw from a piece of ¾″ wood. Drill or whittle out the hole on top (Fig. 1). For sides, cut two pieces of ¼″ wood to fit the shape, which will sandwich in the middle (Fig. 2). Cut a clapper from a piece of an old clothespin 2″ long, or whittle a piece of wood. Drill a small hole in the top of the clapper and tie a string through (Fig. 2). Tie in position on arch shape under hole. Now glue all three pieces together to form the bell shape (Fig. 3).

When dry, whittle and sand the edges even. Add a design. This is a good project for a wood-burning tool, if you like, or carve in the design, being careful not to go too deep. Stain brown.

Nigerian Drum

For a small version of this drum, start with a gallon ice-cream container or similar round container. Cut four pieces of ¼″ thick wood in the size indicated (Fig. 1). Push four tacks through bottom of container, add glue to wood pieces, and attach to bottom by pushing into tacks (Fig. 2). Add glue to other end of wood pieces, push tacks up through lid of container, which now becomes a base, and up into each wood piece (Fig. 2).

For drumhead, find or buy a wooden embroidery hoop about the same diameter as the top of your container. Buy a large sturdy balloon, or use a piece of rubber from an old inflatable beach toy. Ask some friends to help you stretch the rubber. Don't cut the balloon, just stretch over inner ring of embroidery hoop, then slip outside hoop over inner ring to hold taut (Fig. 3).

Tape this drumhead to top of container (Fig. 4). Tape on some crumpled

Drums were an important part of life and ceremony in Africa. Throughout the continent, drums were made in a great variety of shapes and sizes. The simplest was a hollow log with a slit cut in it. These were often huge and their sound carried great distances.

Most dance drums had rawhide heads and a great variety of decorations. The one shown is a huge carved one from southern Nigeria.

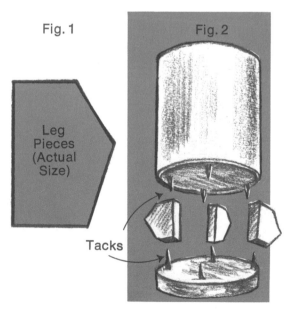

Fig. 1

Leg Pieces (Actual Size)

Fig. 2

Tacks

paper around center of drum to make middle bulge. Then cover with strips of paper dipped in wallpaper paste. Cover edge of hoop to help hold in position, but don't get paste on the rubber (Fig. 5).

Finish with papier-mâché, adding whatever designs you like. This one had geometric designs and a symbol on each side. Using drawing as guide (Fig. 6), shape the symbol in papier-mâché about ¼″ thick. Stick on side of drum. When dry, paint drum brown.

Large drums were usually beaten with the hands, but this one is small for this method. (The original was 4 feet high.) A convenient drumstick for you would be a ½″ styrofoam ball glued to a ¼″ dowel or pencil (Fig. 7).

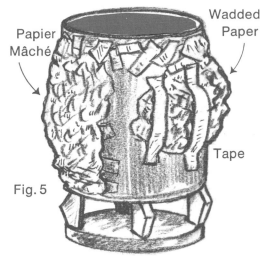

Papier Mâché

Wadded Paper

Tape

Fig. 5

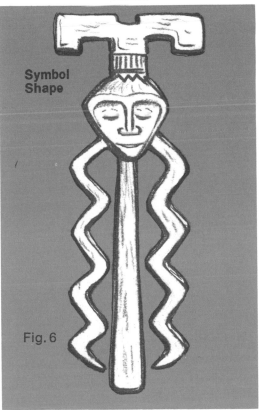

Symbol Shape

Fig. 6

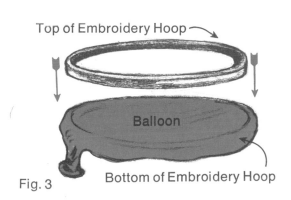

Top of Embroidery Hoop

Balloon

Bottom of Embroidery Hoop

Fig. 3

Fig. 4

Fig. 7

Drumstick

Baulé Drum

This tall Baulé drum was covered with carved figures of all sorts including snakes, human faces, and lizards. Various fetishes (an object with magical meanings), shells, cocoons, and stones were tied on. The Baulé believed all these things added to the power of the drum.

Make this drum from two oatmeal boxes (or salt boxes for a smaller one). Tape together (Fig. 1). Make a drumhead to fit top from balloon and hoops (see previous page). Add papier-mâché all around boxes, building out slightly toward top and around base to get shape shown (Fig. 2). Tie three rows of rope or cord around top, two more at bottom (Fig. 3). Make lizard and snake shape of ¼″ thick papier-mâché and stick on sides (Fig. 4).

When dry, paint dark brown and paint on additional designs in black and white. Add any extra fetishes you like. This will make it your own personal drum. For instance, take a pebble you like, place it in a small piece of old nylon stocking, gather stocking around, and tuck fetish into rope at top of drum (Fig. 4).

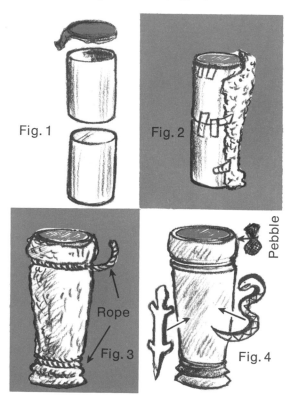

Fig. 1

Fig. 2

Fig. 3 Rope

Fig. 4 Pebble

Double Drum

A skillful drummer could produce many tones from this double-headed drum of Nigeria. It was narrow toward the center. The drumheads were held on by lacings. Thus when the lacings were pressed inward, the tension was increased on the drumheads, changing the tone of the drum. It was carried by a strap over the shoulder and hit with a curved drumstick.

You can make a drum that looks similar, but making one that changes tones is difficult.

Glue and tape together two plastic flower pots 4″ in diameter at tops (Fig. 1). Cover with a thin layer of papier-mâché. When dry, paint light brown.

From a craft or music store purchase a set of bongo drumheads. Soak in water. Lace with wet cords, making sure holes are not directly opposite each other. Cover both open ends of flower pots (Fig. 2). When you have laced all around loosely, begin to tighten tops by pulling laces up. Pull back and forth on laces, going around several times until the laces are as tight as possible (Fig. 3). Allow to dry.

For a drumstick, find a curved stick about 8″ long. Sand smooth, add a small knob at the end, made of plastic, wood, or clay (Fig. 4).

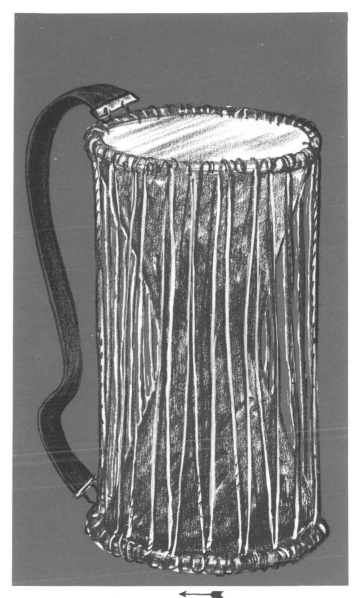

Fig. 1

Fig. 2

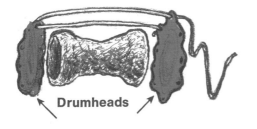

Drumheads

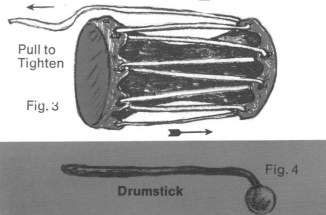

Pull to Tighten

Fig. 3

Drumstick

Fig. 4

Harps

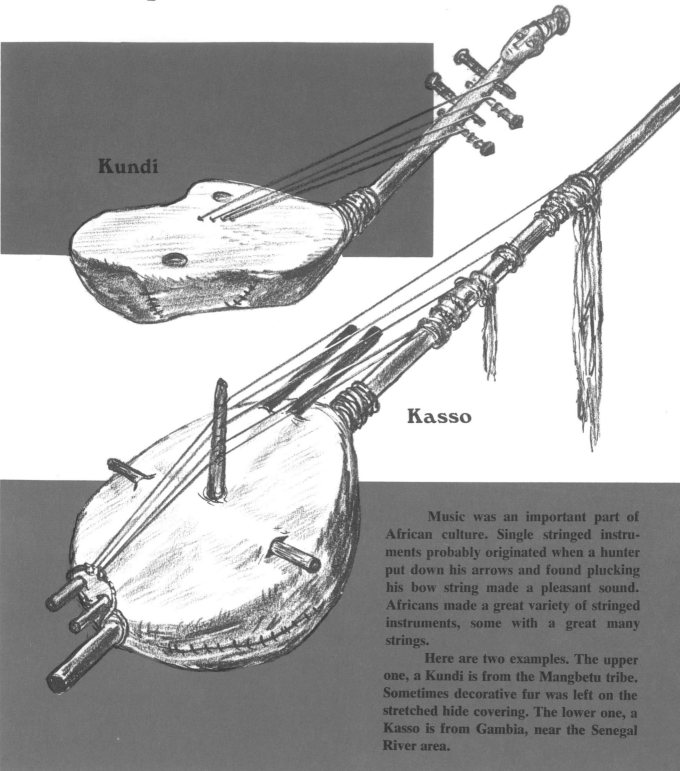

Kundi

Kasso

Music was an important part of African culture. Single stringed instruments probably originated when a hunter put down his arrows and found plucking his bow string made a pleasant sound. Africans made a great variety of stringed instruments, some with a great many strings.

Here are two examples. The upper one, a Kundi is from the Mangbetu tribe. Sometimes decorative fur was left on the stretched hide covering. The lower one, a Kasso is from Gambia, near the Senegal River area.

To make an instrument something like the Kasso, use a plastic gallon bleach bottle. Cut off handle and cut sides of bottle as shown (Fig. 1). Place smaller piece with the handle hole in it at the bottom, and tape in position (Fig. 2). Cut a broomstick, or ¾″ diameter dowel, 30″ long. Push through neck of bottle. Cut a notch in base of bottle to fit stick. Continue to push through and out of handle hole, now at the bottom (Fig. 3).

To make broomstick firm, stuff some paste-soaked paper around neck. Stain the ends of the broomstick outside of the bottle dark brown.

To make a bridge, cut a ½″ dowel 8″ long. Cut four angled notches into this dowel, ending about 2″ down from top (Fig. 4). Position this dowel (bridge) against broomstick (Fig. 5). Flatten sides of dowel and broomstick where they meet.

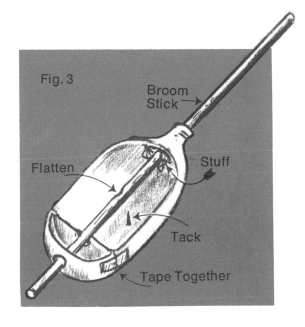

Fig. 3

Broom Stick

Flatten

Stuff

Tack

Tape Together

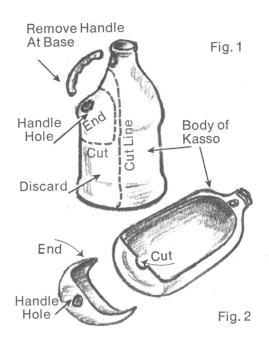

Remove Handle At Base

Fig. 1

Handle Hole

End

Body of Kasso

Cut Line

Cut

Discard

End

Cut

Handle Hole

Fig. 2

BRIDGE

Fig. 4

Notches

Flatten

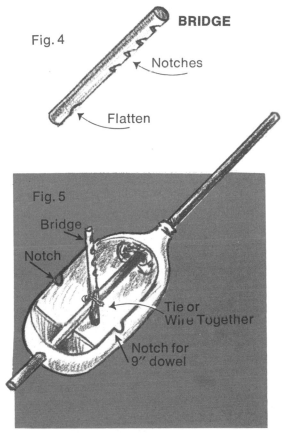

Fig. 5

Bridge

Notch

Tie or Wire Together

Notch for 9″ dowel

Harps continued

Glue and wire together firmly. Push a thumbtack up through bottle into bottom end of this dowel (bridge) where it hits the plastic (Fig. 5). This keeps it from shifting.

For framework, cut ¼″ dowels, two 14″ long and one 9″ long. Cut two notches ¼″ into bottle sides, halfway along the side (Fig. 5). The 9″ dowel will rest in these notches when the leather covering is in place.

Soak a piece of chamois in water, wring out. Make a small hole near center and push the ½″ vertical dowel (bridge)

up through. Wrap chamois around the plastic bottle shape and sew in back, stretching as you go. Sew with wet raffia, if desired, for extra tightness. Continue up and over neck (Fig. 6). As you sew, before it becomes too tight, insert the other dowels you have cut. Make small holes in the chamois and push the two 14″ dowels in place as shown (Fig. 7). Insert them in position parallel with the broomstick, but to the left about 1″ apart. Then slide the 9″ dowel under the two 14″ dowels, across the bottle. Fit this 9″ dowel into the small notches that you cut before. Then continue sewing and tightening the chamois after

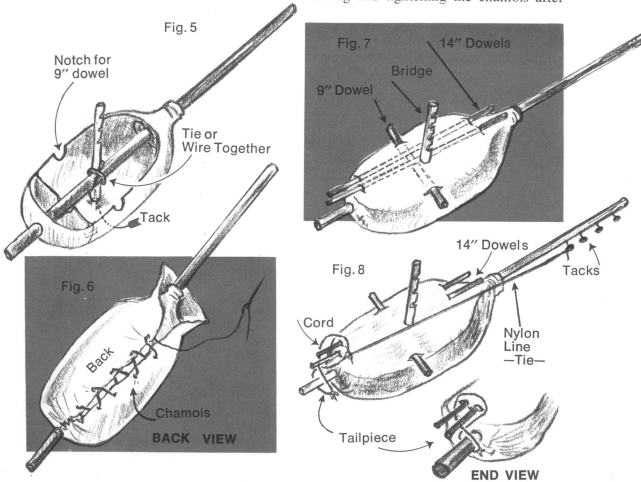

Fig. 5

Notch for 9″ dowel

Tie or Wire Together

Tack

Fig. 6

Back

Chamois

BACK VIEW

Fig. 7   14″ Dowels

Bridge

9″ Dowel

Fig. 8   14″ Dowels

Tacks

Cord

Nylon Line —Tie—

Tailpiece

END VIEW

the dowels are in place. Secure sewing thread and allow to dry.

For tail piece, cut and soak a sturdy cord about 13″ long. Tie this cord in a figure-eight shape around base of broomstick, then up, across, and around the ends of the two dowels (Fig 8). Make it tight.

Place four thumbtacks at even intervals along upper end of broomstick (Fig. 8). For strings, use medium weight nylon fishing line (or old nylon guitar strings). Tie string to cord tail piece at the bottom of the Kasso and up to tacks at top of broomstick. Cut four strings, tying one to each thumbtack. Tie tightly. When all four are tied, pull up the strings one at a time and slip into the notches on the vertical dowel (bridge) (Fig. 9). Stain all ends of dowels that show. Wrap coarse rope around handle to hide the thumbtacks.

The Mangbetu made their Kundi with tuning pegs. Make instrument the same on the Kasso up to Fig. 9. Instead of thumbtacks, drill holes in broomstick and insert 2″ pieces of ¼″ dowel to tie the strings to (Fig. 10). Tie strings on pegs and raise up on bridge as before.

The top had a carved head. Use pattern below as guide. Carve out of balsa wood. Carve hole in base. Insert and glue on the end of the broomstick. Stain dark brown.

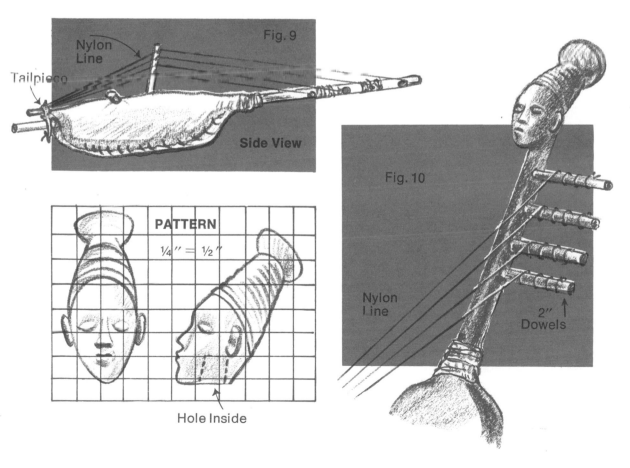

Fig. 9

Nylon Line

Tailpiece

Side View

PATTERN

¼″ = ½″

Hole Inside

Fig. 10

Nylon Line

2″ Dowels

Chi Wara

The Bambara tribe of Mali believed a great buck was sent to teach men how to farm. The carved antelope symbolizes fertility and is tied to a basketlike cap worn on the head during special dance ceremonies to insure good crops and harvest. These lovely stylized figures are often as much as four feet high. Similar carvings show the doe with a baby on her back.

The originals were carved from a single piece of wood. However it will be easier for you to carve the pieces separately and assemble them.

Enlarge patterns (Fig. 1). Trace head and neck on a sheet of ¼" balsa wood. For body, use a block of balsa 8" x 2½" x 2". Trace ears on ¼" thick piece and horns on ½". Carve shapes. Round the horns. Carve or incise crosshatch design on curves of neck and a row along body and on head above eye on both

PATTERNS   ½" = 1½"

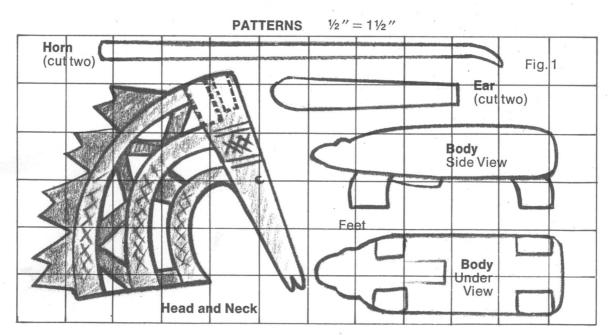

Horn (cut two)

Ear (cut two)

Fig. 1

Body Side View

Feet

Body Under View

Head and Neck

sides (Fig. 2). (A wood-burring tool will give this effect easily.)

For body and legs, trace pattern on block. Cut up between legs with a coping saw. Whittle out shapes of legs and round body. Shape tail area.

Glue feet to a block of pine 7″ x 2½″ x ½″ (Fig. 3). Glue on ears and horns. When dry, attach to body. For strength, first insert 1″ pieces of wire (pieces of paper clip) into the body. Add glue and push neck down in place (Fig. 4).

Stain a dark brown. Give a coat of black paste shoe polish. Polish (Fig. 5). Glue on two black beads for eyes.

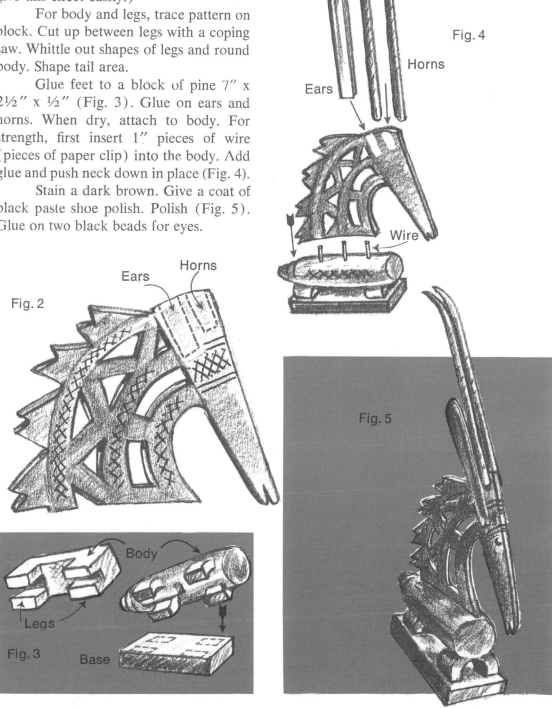

Fig. 4

Horns

Ears

Wire

Fig. 2

Ears

Horns

Fig. 5

Body

Legs

Fig. 3

Base

Ivory Leopard of Benin

The empire of Benin flourished from the thirteenth to the sixteenth centuries. Benin crafts showed highly developed techniques. The leopard was a symbol of royal power. This one was carved of ivory and inlaid with copper spots. The craftsmen of Benin also made exceptionally fine bronze statues of leopards and other animals. Elaborate and intricately detailed groups of figures for statues, door panels, and other decorations were cast in bronze and other metals.

To make the leopard, enlarge pattern. Cut the shape from a sheet of 2½" thick styrofoam with a coping saw. Cut various sections separately if you have only smaller pieces of styrofoam. Using a knife, trim body round, and shape other contours to look like picture. Cut areas between legs (Fig. 1). Add ears and tail later.

Mix a fairly large quantity of clay tinted a pale yellow to look like ivory. Work clay into styrofoam. Cover and decorate a small area at a time. Build up at least ¼" thickness. Round out forms where necessary. Smooth surface with wet fingers.

To get texture, press a decorative button or old earring into the clay before

it hardens. Entire body should be textured (Fig. 2). For the brass spots, poke upholstery tacks with decorative heads in the center of each pressed design (Fig. 3), or paint on copper-colored spots after clay has dried. Make even rows, up over head, around body, down legs. Continue adding clay, pressing in design, and adding tacks until all surfaces and tail are covered.

For face, use a knife to shape mouth in the clay. Roll teeth and tongue of clay and press into position (Fig. 4). Shape eyes. Cut styrofoam ears and cover with clay, pressing in design shown. Press ears against head and blend clay around to hold. Add a wire in end of tail, poke into body, add glue to attach tail.

When clay is dry, paint outline and center of eyes black. String red tubettini and tie around body just in front of the back legs.

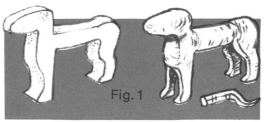

Fig. 1

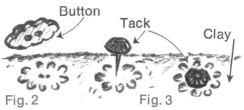

Button
Tack
Clay

Fig. 2   Fig. 3

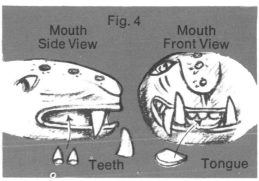

Fig. 4

Mouth
Side View

Mouth
Front View

Teeth   Tongue

PATTERN

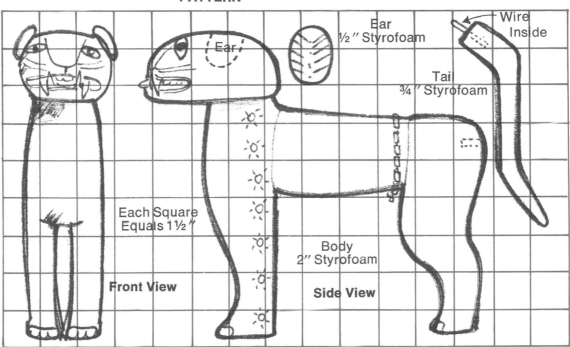

Ear

Ear
½" Styrofoam

Wire
Inside

Tail
¾" Styrofoam

Each Square
Equals 1½"

Front View

Body
2" Styrofoam

Side View

Bakota Naja Figure

The decorative heads on the baskets which held the bones of ancestors of the Bakota tribe of Gabon, often had decorative narrow strips of copper on the face, sometimes feather decorations in back. The Bakota also made another version of this figure called the Mbulu-Ngulu, which was entirely covered with thin layers of brass or copper. A stylized shape at the back replaced the feathers.

Begin with a basket about 8″ in diameter and 4″ to 6″ high. Cut a piece of heavy cardboard to fit 1″ down inside the basket (Fig. 1). Enlarge patterns on opposite page. Cut shape shown for base and neck out of 1″ thick wood, or cut from cardboard and add thickness with papier-mâché. Round neck and shape (Fig. 2). Cut head from ½″ balsa wood, shape. Stain both pieces with black and brown shoe polish. Using small screws, glue and attach neck section to the cardboard circle (Fig. 3).

Cut reeds long enough to make handles. Poke holes in cardboards and adjust height (Fig. 4) so reeds extend ½″ below platform. Tie a string around each end underneath and add glue to hold at proper height (Fig. 5).

To make face, cut strips of aluminum foil ½″ wide. Fold in thirds and fold again. Fold under ends and glue with household cement to make decorations on face (Fig. 6). First do the chin and eyebrow strips, then cover ends with cheek strips. Crumple round shapes of foil for eyes and glue on (Fig. 7). Cut ears from an aluminum foil plate, fold edge, and glue on.

Collect some feathers from a feather duster, old hats, etc. Cut a notch in neck section. Glue feathers in position and glue face over this. You may need to notch back of face also to make room for the feathers. Weight down until glue dries (Fig. 8).

PATTERNS   Each Square = 1″

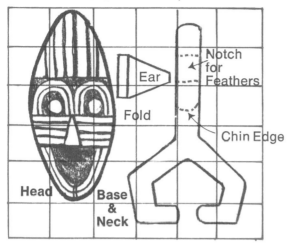

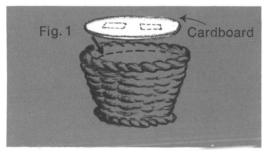

Fig. 1   Cardboard

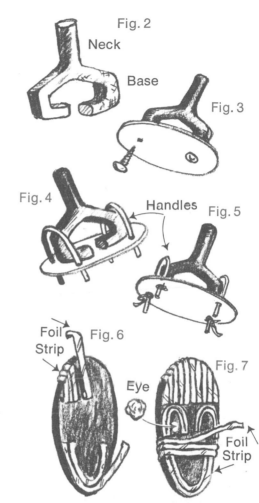

Fig. 2   Neck   Base   Fig. 3

Fig. 4   Handles   Fig. 5

Foil Strip   Fig. 6   Eye   Fig. 7   Foil Strip

For nose, cut a small wedge-shaped piece of wood the proper size, cover with aluminum foil and glue in position. Wind folded strips of ¼″ wide aluminum foil around neck section and glue. (See illustration.)

The basket was covered with woven grass. You can find this type of straw in old beach hats or bags. Or you can use pieces of coarsely-woven fabric. Cut to fit around top of basket, dampen, and shape. Hold straw in position with clothespins while drying. Sew on if necessary. Glue on straw strips to cover handles. Braid strips of raffia or tan crepe paper and attach to straw so strips hang down, covering basket.

Museums often display these heads without the basket. If you prefer, make only the head and neck section.

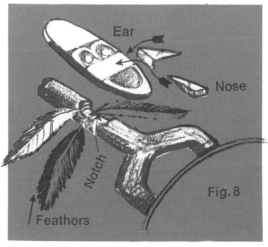

Ear   Nose   Notch   Feathers   Fig. 8

Mask of "Do"

These masks of the Bobo tribe were used in dance ceremonies and were often as much as five feet tall. The dancer was completely covered by a grass costume. Many dancers, holding such masks, participated. (This one is shown sitting, waiting his turn.)

Dõ was a guardian spirit. The prong or horn that protruded from the forehead was to impale witches. This mask and the accompanying dance vanquished anything that disturbed the peacefulness of the tribe.

Similar masks that were horizontal represented butterflies, the first sign of spring and growth.

Cut a long piece of cardboard 36" x 8" wide from the side of a large corrugated box. Following pattern on opposite page, cut shapes at top and bottom. Cut out the two triangular shapes near the center. Paint white. When dry, draw horizontal and vertical lines 1" apart, making squares. Color in a black and red checkerboard effect. Draw diagonals in top, center, and base sections, forming triangles. Color the triangles black.

For head, use two 7" paper plates or cut two cardboard circles. Paint white. Decorate one as the face. Glue on black cord in circles for eyes or paint black circles. For nose, cut a styrofoam cup down to 1". Paint cut edge black. Glue in position. Paint in other details of the face in black (Fig. 1).

Overlap two yardsticks and glue behind long shape as shown (Fig. 2). The lower end of the stick is to hold the mask. Glue plate with face on it to the yardstick, in front, just below long shape. Glue other plate behind face plate and in back of the

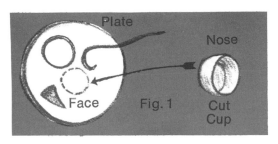

Plate · Nose · Face · Cut Cup

Fig. 1

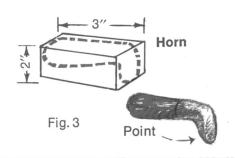

3″ · 2″

Horn

Fig. 3

Point

yardstick. Staple edges of the plates together to hold securely.

Protruding from the design, just above the face, is a wooden shape like a horn. Cut it out of ¾″ balsa wood (Fig. 3). Round off edges and taper to a point. Paint red at the base and black near the tip. Glue or nail in position as indicated on pattern.

To complete the costume, use an old sheet. Drape over the head, mark where eye and hand holes are needed. Cut off extra at bottom edge. Remove and cut out holes. Using red, yellow, or brown felt-tipped markers, draw on a grass texture (Fig. 4).

PATTERN

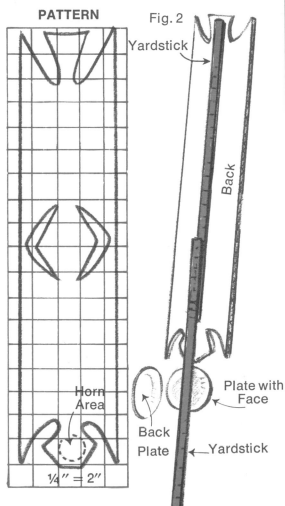

Fig. 2

Yardstick

Back

Horn Area

Plate with Face

Back Plate

Yardstick

¼″ = 2″

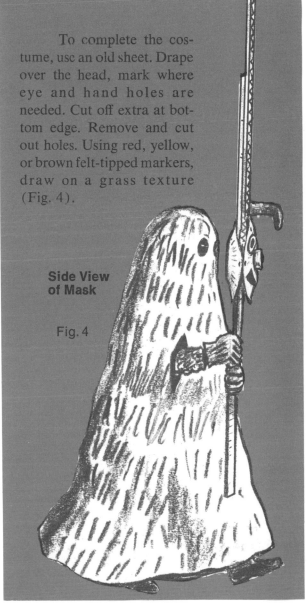

Side View of Mask

Fig. 4

Poro Mask

Masks were carved of wood in many shapes. Not all masks went in front of the face or partly around the head; some rested above the head, either vertical or at an angle. The head of the wearer, and often the entire body, was covered with cloth or grasses. Frequent ceremonies were a part of tribal life.

This mask from the Dan tribe of Liberia was used by the Poro Society. Rituals in this men's secret society perpetuated the ancestors and the customs of the tribe and initiated young men into manhood. This mask was inlaid with metal teeth and eyes. Dances were sometimes performed on stilts.

Especially sacred were small duplicates of this mask about four inches high, worn by the initiated.

Enlarge the pattern on the opposite page. For base shape, use a paper platter or a piece of cardboard the proper size. Cut pieces of cardboard, wood, or styrofoam the proper size and shape for nose and mouth. Make papier-mâché as described in the introduction. Put on a layer about ¼″ thick, building up more toward center. As cardboard becomes soft curve it slightly so mask will fit around your face better. With paste strips attach nose and mouth. Shape papier-mâché around them.

Before it dries, cut slits for eyes and two nostril holes (Fig. 1). Smooth surface with wet fingers. Place on a curved surface that will help maintain the curved shape and allow to dry thoroughly.

This basic procedure can be used for most all simple face masks of this type. If you find a picture of one you like, make it this way, shaping and coloring it to look like your picture.

Paint this Poro mask a greenish-tan. Antique it if you wish (see introduction).

PATTERN

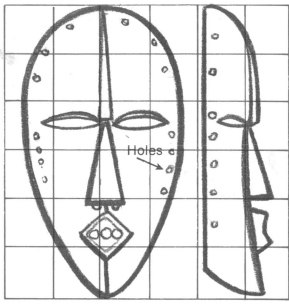

$\frac{1}{2}'' = 2''$

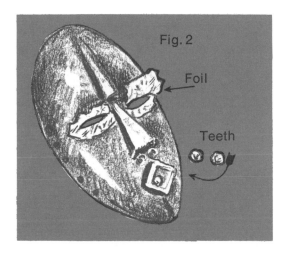

Fig. 2

Foil

Teeth

Make some beads of clay. The ones for the string under the chin should be about ¾″ long and ¼″ in diameter. Color the clay or paint purple and blue (Fig. 4). Make about fifty. For the top piece you'll need one hundred or more beads about ⅜″ around. Purchase these beads, use old necklaces if you have some, or make out of clay. The beads should be mostly white with some red and some blue. If making them of clay, string on a wire or skewer and allow to dry thoroughly (Fig. 5).

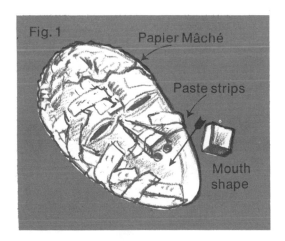

Fig. 1

Papier Mâché

Paste strips

Mouth shape

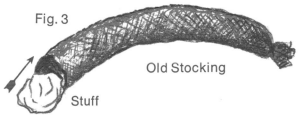

Fig. 3

Old Stocking

Stuff

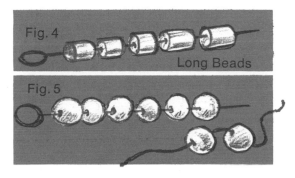

Fig. 4

Long Beads

Fig. 5

When dry, cut four 1″ x 4″ pieces of aluminum foil. Crumple and fit into and around eye holes. Glue in position with household cement. Crumple three small balls of foil and glue on for teeth (Fig. 2).

For decorative piece over top, cut an old nylon stocking 20″ x 4″, fold over cut edges, and sew together, making a tube about 1½″ in diameter (Fig. 3). Stuff with old stockings or cotton.

Poro Mask continued

With a heavy thread, string the ⅜″ beads and loop around the stuffed nylon piece. Stitch through underneath at intervals to hold (Fig. 6). Use another needle and a finer thread to sew along top, catching beads and holding them in proper position. Keep most of the beads toward the front where they will look best above mask.

String the long beads on two cords about 16″ long. With an awl, make holes on sides and top (see pattern). Through these holes, attach the two rows of beads to hang about chin level. Also attach the top piece by tying cords to ends of nylon piece and then tying through holes. Using 12″ pieces of coarse twine or thin rope, tie on two purchased bells about 3″ long (Fig. 7). Find two pieces of metal (old bolts will do), spray copper. Tie a cord on each and tie into holes at each side of mask so they hang just behind the bells.

For hanging on the wall or when you wear it, tie a 15″ cord in the holes on both sides of mask (Fig. 7).

Rub face sparingly with gold antiquing.

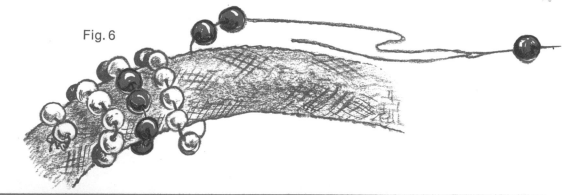

Fig. 6

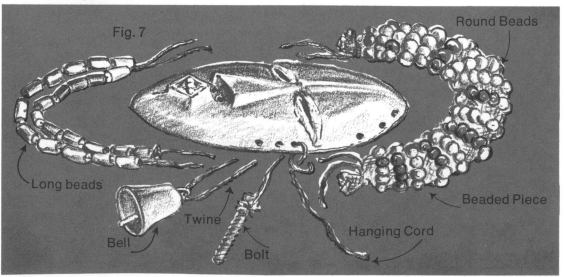

Fig. 7

Round Beads

Long beads

Bell

Twine

Bolt

Beaded Piece

Hanging Cord

Ikenga

Each man of the Ibo tribe owned such a carved figure signifying his life, fortune, and strength. Its size depended on the importance of the owner. Some were only a few inches high; others were almost life-sized. The horns represented good luck. The Ikenga was often consulted and given offerings for success in trade, farming, and hunting.

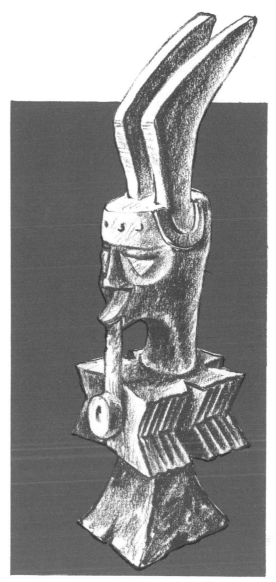

Each Square = 1″

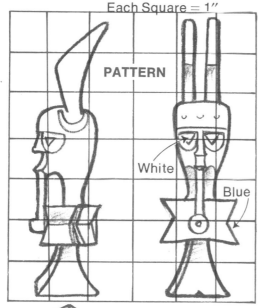

PATTERN

White

Blue

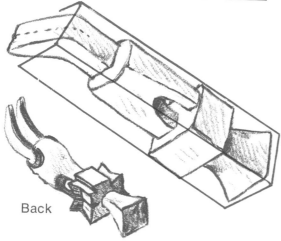

Back

Enlarge pattern and trace onto a piece of balsa wood 7″ x 2″ x 2″. Cut away excess areas with a coping saw. Carve finer details. Refer to pattern often to get proper proportions.

Paint eyes and edges of design white and blue. The original probably was painted blue, but most of the paint has worn off.

Paint remainder brown. Go over with black shoe polish to give it a sheen. Now you have your own Ikenga.

Porpianong (Bird Headdress)

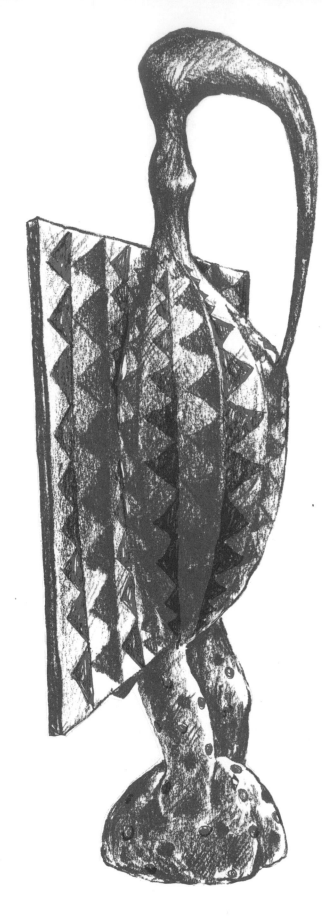

This headdress showed a sacred mythological bird called the porpianong, which was a symbol of life force or basic elements. The Senufo tribe carved these wooden figures four to five feet high. Despite the size of the figure, the base was hollow so it could be worn on the head during rituals. The Senufo believed this bird to be one of the first five creatures on earth. It was also believed to carry the souls of the dead to the next world.

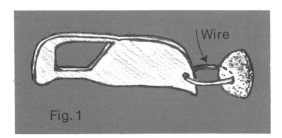

Fig. 1

To make a miniature about 15″ high, enlarge pattern on opposite page. Cut profile shape from cardboard or ¼″ balsa wood. Cut two wings of ¼″ balsa wood 7″ x 2¾″. For base, cut a 2″ styrofoam ball in half. Bend a 7″ piece of wire to go up through the body and down through the ball (Fig. 1).

Now build up rounded forms. Add wads of paper for belly and to round head and neck. Tape on and add strips of paper dipped in paste. Wind strips around wire legs to give thickness and hold in position (Fig. 2). Check areas where wings attach and keep flat, but add wings later.

PATTERN

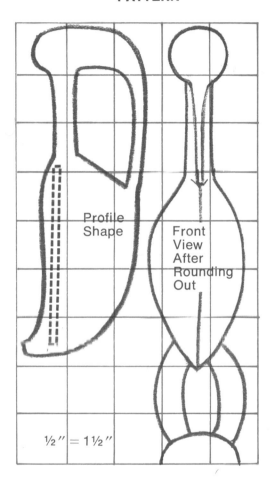

Profile Shape

Front View After Rounding Out

½″ = 1½″

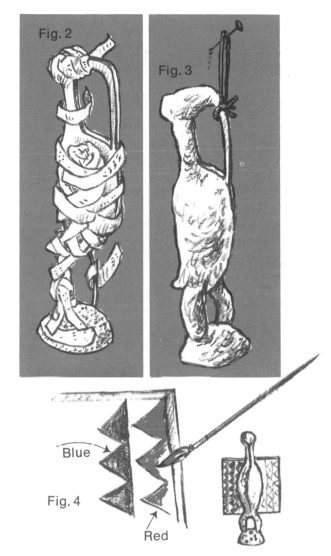

Fig. 2

Fig. 3

Blue

Fig. 4

Red

You may need several layers of papier-mâché to build up proper shape and make legs firm. Allow to dry between layers. Put a thin layer over base also. To allow legs to dry in proper position, it may help to suspend the bird by the beak while papier-mâché is drying (Fig. 3). When dry, glue on wings. Add more papier-mâché if necessary to fit wings and get proper shape.

Paint head and down neck a brown-black. Cover remainder with white latex paint. When dry, draw on a zig-zag pattern. Color in alternate rows of red and blue triangles over body and wings (Fig. 4). Dab red and blue dots on base. A drop of white glue added to water-color paint will help make it waterproof. When dry, cover with a dark wood stain and immediately wipe it all off. Enough paint will remain in the crevices to make the object look old and weathered.

Dogon Masks

Rabbit

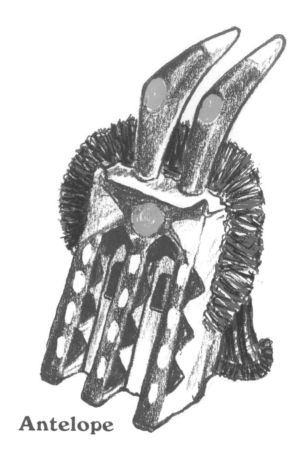

Antelope

These masks of a men's secret society had many variations of the basic square shape. Horns and pointed ears symbolized the antelope; rounded ears, the rabbit. Sometimes a three-feet-high, cross-like shape was attached on top, symbolizing certain birds.

The rabbit appeared in many folk tales and may have been the ancestor of our mischievous, wily "Br'er Rabbit."

Start construction of basic shape with a shoe box and three tops from 12″ long molded egg cartons. Cut eye holes in the bottom of the box (Fig. 1). Cut one egg carton cover 1½″ down from one end. Cut this 10½″ piece in half lengthwise (Fig. 2). Fit covers around shoe box as shown (Fig. 3). Full covers go at sides of box, partial cover on top. Tape in position.

Using the shoe box cover, mark areas shown (Fig. 4). Cut, fold, and tape piece to box (Fig. 5) with forehead over eyes. Cover entire shape with strips of paper dipped in thin wallpaper paste. Fill in areas across the forehead and curve slightly over eyes and around nose (Fig. 6). Hide all tapes with a thin layer of papier-mâché.

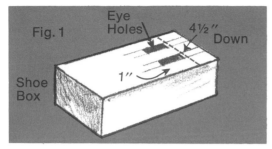

Fig. 1

Eye Holes

4½″ Down

1″

Shoe Box

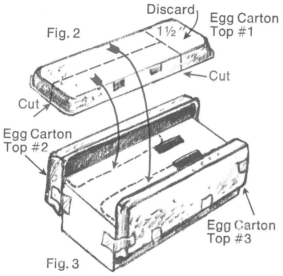

Fig. 2

Discard

1½″

Egg Carton Top #1

Cut

Cut

Egg Carton Top #2

Egg Carton Top #3

Fig. 3

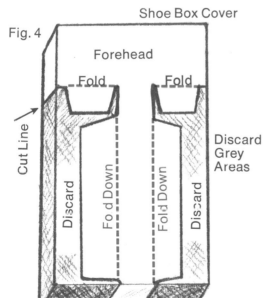

Fig. 4

Shoe Box Cover

Forehead

Fold

Fold

Cut Line

Discard

Fold Down

Fold Down

Discard

Discard Grey Areas

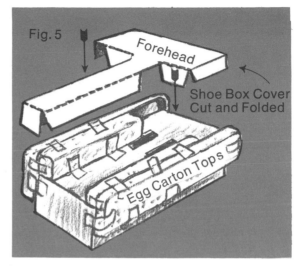

Fig. 5

Forehead

Shoe Box Cover Cut and Folded

Egg Carton Tops

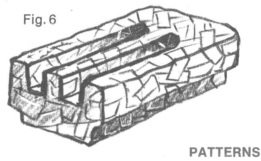

Fig. 6

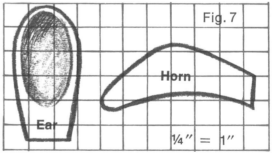

PATTERNS

Fig. 7

Horn

Ear

¼″ = 1″

Cut ears (or horns) out of piece of styrofoam ¾″ thick (Fig. 7). To hold ears in place, push a nail up from inside of the box and push ears onto it (Fig. 8). Continue papier-mâché up and over ears, covering surface and holding them in place. Entire mask and ears should have about ¼″ layer of papier-mâché over it when finished.

Dogon Masks continued

When dry, paint white. For rabbit mask, paint on brown dots, pink in ears and around eyes (see illustration on previous page). For antelope, color in blue triangles around face, pink spots on forehead, and blue horns with pink spots (Fig. 9).

For decorative fringe around mask, cut a piece of red or orange upholstery edging 21″ long. Place up and around the mask. Tape or sew on (Fig. 9).

The back of the head was covered with a piece of striped fabric. Cut a piece 15″ x 24″. Add a fringed edge. Attach to back of mask at top with tape (Fig. 10). Add ties at each side.

The costume worn with this mask consisted of grass tufts tied at the wrists, elbows, and ankles, and a knee-length grass skirt. Use raffia or crepe paper cut in thin strips to get this effect. Measure length needed. Cut several layers of the proper size, then cut in narrow strips nearly to the edge. Sew uncut edge to a fabric tape, leaving ties on ends (Fig. 11). Sew on several layers. Tie around figure. Chest piece was made of knotted rope with a grass fringe (Fig. 12).

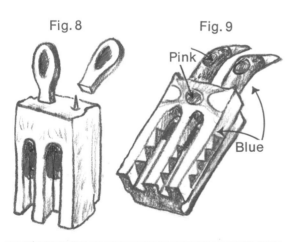

Fig. 8

Fig. 9

Pink

Blue

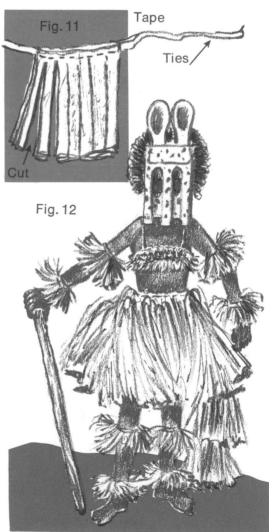

Fig. 11

Tape

Ties

Cut

Fig. 12

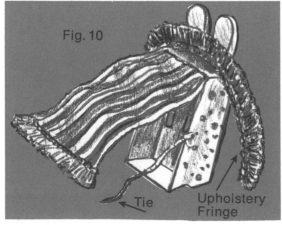

Fig. 10

Tie

Upholstery Fringe

Clothing : Zulu

The craft of weaving had been known there for many centuries. Today a mixture of traditional and western clothing is most commonly seen.

In the Zulu tribe, elaborate clothing was for special occasions only. Everyday clothes were simple and brief. Only the chief was allowed to wear the leopard skin necklace and claws. It was believed the ferocity of the animal would be transferred to the chief when he wore them.

There was a great variety in traditional dress of each tribal area. To the north, clothing showed nomad and Arab influence in the turbans and long robes. Farther south, in the hot climates, clothing was practically nonexistent. Clothing styles also varied throughout the centuries. For example, in the medieval kingdom of Ghana, court costumes were opulent, made of many rich materials and patterns.

Zulu Clothing continued

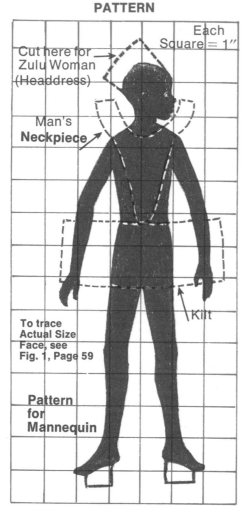

PATTERN

Each Square = 1"

Cut here for Zulu Woman (Headdress)

Man's **Neckpiece**

Kilt

To trace Actual Size Face, see Fig. 1, Page 59

Pattern for Mannequin

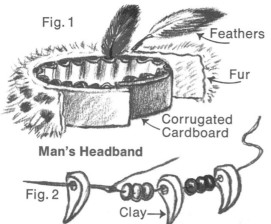

Fig. 1

Feathers

Fur

Corrugated Cardboard

Man's Headband

Fig. 2

Clay →

First make a silhouette mannequin to display the costume you'll make. Enlarge pattern on this page. Cut out of heavy cardboard or ¼" balsa wood. Paint black. Push tab below feet into a chunk of clay to hold upright.

Men wore animals' skins in many ways. Make a pattern for kilt and neckpiece that fit around this figure. Cut from fake-fur fabric or draw leopard design on cotton fabric with felt-tipped markers. Sew or pin in back to hold.

For headband, cut a piece of flexible corrugated cardboard ½" wide to fit around head. Tape around head with corrugations on inside. Glue on a piece of furry fabric. Insert small feathers or feather pieces into corrugations (Fig. 1). For knee decorations, string several strands of beads and wrap around legs as shown on previous page. Glue. Hang a bit of unraveled, coarse rope 3" long from this knee band to look like lion fur. (Zulus also hung lions' manes from the waist and sometimes from the armbands.)

For around neck, make four claw shapes of clay ⅜" long. Make holes for stringing. When dry, string three beads of various colors between each claw. Make long enough to fit neck (Fig. 2).

For the woman, cut mannequin with head shaped for headdress, dotted line on pattern. Loop several strands of beads around wrists and upper arms, several more around below knees and around ankles. Use old beads, colored tubettini, *etc*. Glue in back if necessary. Make several necklaces also. For flat neckpiece, cut a piece of fabric larger than area needed. Draw on design about 1" x ¾" (Fig. 3).

Sew on beads (Fig. 4). String three beads, sew down into fabric, string three more, sew down, and so on. Continue laying rows of beads evenly and tight to each other. When complete, tie thread. Saturate back of fabric with thinned white glue. When dry, trim close to beads. Add larger beads at either side and attach around neck (Fig. 5).

Make headband in same manner, beading area about ¼″ wide and long enough to fit around head. Glue in position. Above beaded band, wind red yarn, glueing edges as you go to make a flat, even effect. Paint three toothpicks white. Glue a few beads to ends of toothpicks and tuck into yarn (Fig. 6). Make a striped

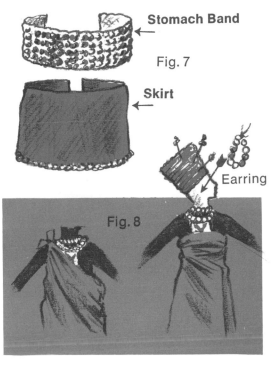

Stomach Band

Fig. 7

Skirt

Fig. 8

Earring

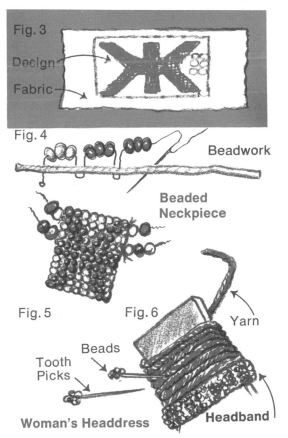

Fig. 3

Design

Fabric

Fig. 4

Beadwork

Beaded Neckpiece

Fig. 5   Fig. 6   Yarn

Beads

Tooth Picks

Woman's Headdress   **Headband**

beaded band (same procedure as above) about ⅝″ wide and long enough to go around stomach. For skirt, cut red cotton fabric about 1¾″ x 4″. Add a narrow beaded edge, place around figure, and secure both in back (Fig. 7).

Outer garment is red or brown cotton 10″ square, either knotted over one shoulder or tucked under the arms (Fig. 8). String two small loops of beads and attach for earrings.

These could be made into full size costumes by enlarging sizes. Measure lengths and distance around to fit your size. Make patterns of brown paper to check fit. Cut out fabric or fake furs, using pattern. Make beadwork appropriate size. Neckpiece and headband could be about 3″ wide.

N'Debele Clothing

The N'Debele women fashioned necklaces, armbands, and anklets from woven grasses, solidly beaded. Brass wire bangles encircled the lower arms and legs.

You may wish to make this costume on a doll or display it on the mannequin described on the preceding page.

For beaded necklace, cut a piece of clothesline to fit around neck. Sew ends together (Fig. 1). Using a bead needle, string white or blue seed beads. Wind around, stitching through rope on every third loop (Fig. 2). Continue adding beads. Add dab of glue if they slip. Beads should solidly cover rope.

For elbow and calf, repeat, making four beaded pieces the proper size to fit. On arm, starting just below the beaded band, wind a piece of silver or gold cord (gift-wrap tie). Glue down starting end, wrap evenly, and tuck other end in and glue near wrist. Repeat on leg as shown (Fig. 3). It would be difficult to bead smaller bracelets. Instead, wrap a pipe cleaner around each wrist and ankle. Wrap several times to build up desired thickness to look like beaded band. Use red, white, green, and blue (Fig. 4).

For beaded headband, cut a 10″ piece of picture wire. Using pliers, pull out two strands of this fine wire. String one blue bead and three white beads. Put one blue bead on second wire. Then put this second wire up through the three white beads (Fig. 5). String one blue bead and three white on top wire, one blue on bottom, and repeat four times (Fig. 6). Now string four blue beads on both wires, then three white on top, and repeat until you have enough to fit around the head (Fig. 7). Twist wires into end where they meet and cut off any excess.

Real coins were often suspended from the headband. Simulate this with flat gold sequins. Poke a hole toward one side, put a small piece of wire through, twist onto the beadwork. Twist on three or four sequins, using a separate piece of wire for each (Fig. 8).

For blanket, cut a square of wool fabric about the same height as your doll, or cut strips of red, yellow, and bright-blue felt. Glue edges to each other to form a square the proper size. Fold corner of red top down at angle as shown (Fig. 9). Wrap around figure (Fig. 10), the un-folded corner coming up over shoulder.

String 1″ of odd shapes and colors of small beads. Tie to a small safety pin (Fig. 11). Pin blanket on shoulder.

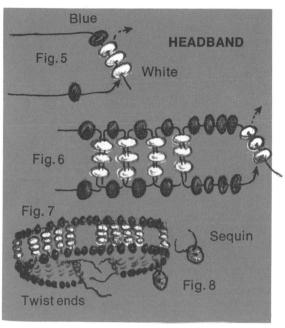

Blue

HEADBAND

Fig. 5

White

Fig. 6

Fig. 7

Sequin

Fig. 8

Twist ends

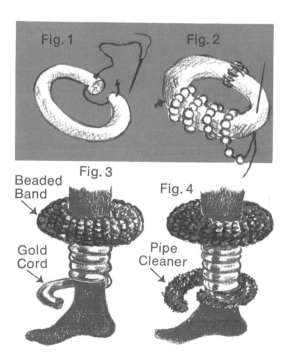

Fig. 1

Fig. 2

Fig. 3

Beaded Band

Fig. 4

Gold Cord

Pipe Cleaner

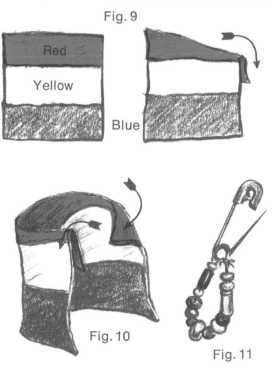

Fig. 9

Red

Yellow

Blue

Fig. 10

Fig. 11

Masai Clothing

The Masai tribe was noted for its cattle raising. The boys used to be initiated into manhood with a lion hunt. On ceremonial occasions they wore an odd headdress of ostrich feathers that surrounded the face. The hair was braided and coated with red mud.

Make this costume for a mannequin as described on a previous page. For Man: Paint on reddish-brown hair (Fig. 1). Cut a piece of brownish-red fabric 6″ x 12″, drape and tie over one shoulder. It should hang about knee length. For wrist and arm decorations string small beads of white with some red and some blue. Wind a couple of strands around each wrist and upper arm. Glue in back. For his earring, take a piece of picture wire (see previous page), string beads to form a triangle with large red bead at the bottom (Fig. 2). Fit over ear, and glue or wire in place.

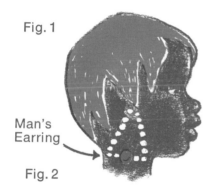

Fig. 1

Man's Earring

Fig. 2

For Woman: Cut fabric 8″ x 12″, tie over shoulder. For wide necklace, make three rows of beads around neck, three plain rows, using gold gift-wrap cord or thin copper wire. Then string three more rows of beads, mostly red and white, some blue. Make each row larger so they will lay smoothly out over shoulders. Using fine wire, make a loop around each strand, from neck out over shoulder on each side to hold all the beads and cords in proper position (Fig. 3).

For vertical beads, use a variety of colorful beads, tubettini, *etc.* String three strands of these beads to hang from center of bottom row of neckpiece. They should hang almost to the knees. Make single strands of small beads around the wrists and ankles.

Use a single strand of picture wire to make one row of beads to fit around head, twist on a row of beads over top. Loop wire to go over and around ears (Fig. 4). From ear loops, suspend several copper wire (or cord) loops to hang to the shoulders. Make loops, slip into ear loop, twist ends. Add a dab of household cement to hold. (Actually, these were huge metal loops that pierced the ears.)

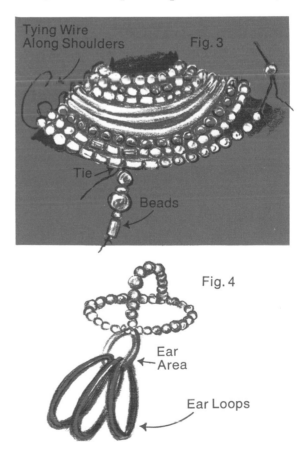

Tying Wire Along Shoulders   Fig. 3

Tie

Beads

Fig. 4

Ear Area

Ear Loops

Shields

MASAI

For the Masai shield, use two kite sticks about 30″ long. For center brace, cut a stick about 11″ long (Fig. 1). Wet sticks slightly, shape in position, and glue together (Fig. 2). Tie, tape, and clamp to hold until thoroughly dry. To keep papier-mâché from falling through frame, tie string back and forth across frame (Fig. 3). Dip wide strips of newsprint in thinned wallpaper paste and fit around to make surface (Fig. 4). Before the papier-mâché dries, attach handle.

For handle, cut piece of a plastic bleach bottle as shown (Fig. 5). Remove the bottle's handle and part of side. Tie string to each end of handle and up to points of shield. Tighten strings so shield front bends forward slightly (Fig. 6). Stick some strips of papier-mâché over base of handle. Allow to dry thoroughly.

Shields were made in a great variety of sizes and shapes. Some only a few inches long were carried in dance rituals and were merely symbols of their original use. Shapes varied from tribe to tribe. In Kenya, shields were quite round with designs painted on the hide. Farther south, the Zulus made more pointed, narrower ones, usually covered with furry-animal skin. In the Cameroons, an irregular shield shape was made of hippopotamus skin.

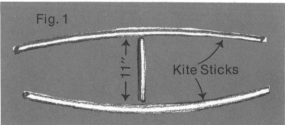

Fig. 1 — 11″ — Kite Sticks

Fig. 2 — Glue

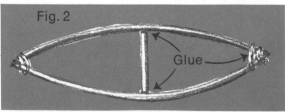

Fig. 3 — String

Paint white, then add designs in red, blue, and black. (Gray areas in the drawing indicate bright blue.)

A round version can be made from a circular toy or plastic hoop. Tie string back and forth (Fig. 3). Add papier-mâché. Paint on similar designs (Fig. 7).

To make Zulu shield shown below, follow steps to Fig. 3. Cut a piece of fake-fur fabric to fit shape. Wrap around edges and glue, holding with clothespins until dry (Fig. 8). Lay a stick about 7″ longer than shield on back (Fig. 9). Poke holes and sew in and out with heavy yarn. This adds decoration in front (Fig. 10) and holds stick in position. Wrap top tip of stick with bright yarn and feathers. Glue.

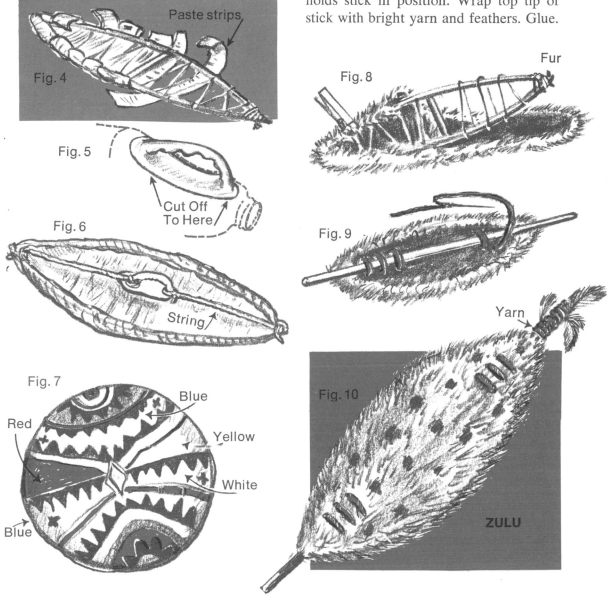

Fig. 4 — Paste strips

Fig. 5 — Cut Off To Here

Fig. 6 — String

Fig. 7 — Blue, Red, Yellow, White, Blue

Fig. 8 — Fur

Fig. 9

Fig. 10 — Yarn — ZULU

Pendants

In the Kingdom of Benin and among the Ashanti and Baulé tribes, gold pendants were made by the lost wax method (described on page 18). Necklaces, rings, armbands, earrings, and other ornaments were skillfully made. It is possible to get more intricate detail with gold than bronze. The Ashanti usually made their shapes from finely-rolled pieces of wax, giving a ridged appearance to the casting. Pendants were often worn by men of rank and hung from a waistband.

Farther south, the Bapende tribe carved miniature masks of ivory, which had ceremonial meanings. Years of use often wore the features smooth.

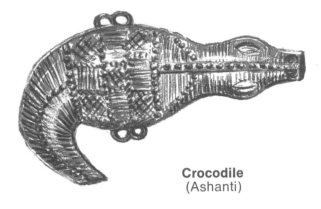

Crocodile
(Ashanti)

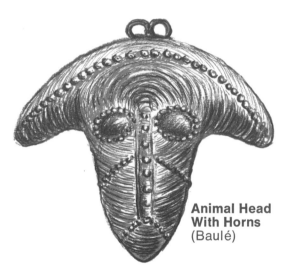

**Animal Head
With Horns**
(Baulé)

Ivory Head
(Bapende)

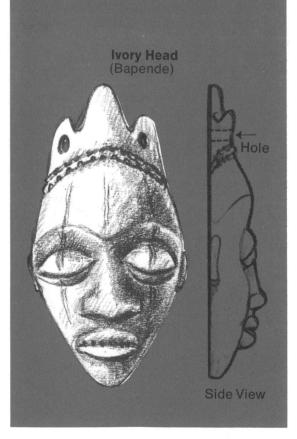

Hole

Side View

To make pattern for the pendant desired trace shapes shown. To make form or mold, use nonhardening commercial clay. Make a flat base, roll a strip of clay, and place around in general contour of the shape you've decided to make. Blend clay down and around into base so sides are smoothly rounded. Push eyes down in with a rounded tool (Fig. 1). Remember you are working in reverse. Whatever you push into the clay, will stick out in the finished piece. The mold should be no more than ¾″ deep (see side view). With a dull pointed stick, scratch the circular textured designs on the animals and decorative edgings on the head. For the crocodile, scratch criss-cross textures on back. Indent rows of dots on animals as shown (Fig. 2). These will look like rows of beads when reversed.

For hanger on crocodile and animal, bend wire in shape as shown (Fig. 3) and push up into clay, leaving lower end in form. For head, push in two short pieces of pipe cleaner at either side on top, standing up. These will form two holes for the head to hang by (Fig. 4).

When your form is completed, mix ⅛ cup water and ⅛ cup of plaster of paris in a paper cup. Pour into form. Let set several hours, then carefully pull away clay. Clean and carve more shape and decorations where necessary. Smooth with fingers or other tools to desired shape. Pull out pipe cleaners.

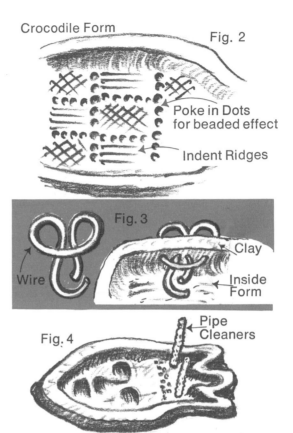

Crocodile Form

Fig. 2

Poke in Dots for beaded effect

Indent Ridges

Fig. 3

Clay

Wire

Inside Form

Fig. 4

Pipe Cleaners

Bapende Head Form

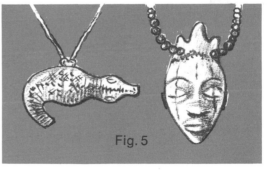

Fig. 5

When dry, spray crocodile and animal gold. Paint Bapende head yellowish white to look like ivory. Finish with a coat of colorless nail polish. Suspend from a necklace of beads. Suspend gold pendants from a chain or cord (Fig. 5).

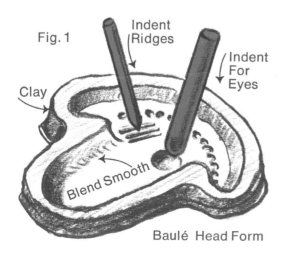

Fig. 1

Indent Ridges

Indent For Eyes

Clay

Blend Smooth

Baulé Head Form

Congo Comb

The Bakuba occupied a large area of the southern Congo. Although they carved many religious and practical items, they are best known for their portrait statues of their long line of kings. The Bakuba and other tribes often used combs as part of decorative hair styling. The one shown was made of wood. Several tribes carved combs and other hair ornaments out of ivory.

Trace body from drawing on the left, which is the actual size of finished comb. Transfer to a piece of ¾″ balsa wood. Cut and carve (Fig. 1). For circular piece for back of head, cut a 2″ circle from balsa wood ⅛″ thick. Carve in zigzag design front and back, or use a woodburning tool to make design.

To make teeth of comb, cut four dowels ³⁄₁₆″ in diameter and 4½″ long. To taper ends, rub on sandpaper.

Carve or drill four holes in the body base. Add glue and insert dowels (Fig. 2). Straighten and allow to dry. Glue on circular headpiece. For decoration around base, glue on three pieces of string or decorative cord as shown. Paint or stain dark brownish-black.

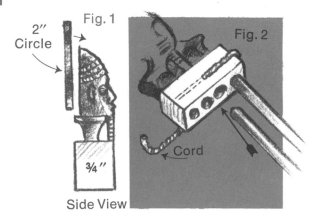

Fig. 1
2″ Circle
¾″
Side View

Fig. 2
Cord

Suggested Further Reading

THE FOLLOWING BOOKS ARE ESPECIALLY FOR YOUNG PEOPLE:

Glubok, Shirley. *The Art of Africa.*
   New York: Harper & Row, 1965.

Kittler, Glenn D. *Let's Travel in the Congo.*
   Chicago: Childrens Press, 1965.

Leuzinger, Elsy. *The Art of Africa.*
   New York: Greystone Press, 1967.

Sutton, Felix. *The Illustrated Book About Africa.*
   New York: Grosset and Dunlap, 1959.

There are also a number of adult books with many illustrations that can be easily appreciated:

Coughlan, Robert. *Tropical Africa.*
   New York: Time Incorporated, 1962.

Davidson, Basil. *African Kingdoms.*
   New York: Time, Inc., 1966.

Elisofon, Eliot. *The Sculpture of Africa.*
   New York: Fredrick N. Praeger, 1958.

Parrinder, Geoffrey. *African Mythology.*
   London: Paul Hamlyn, 1967.

Schmalenbach, Werner. *African Art.*
   New York: Thomas Yoseloff, 1960.

Mail Order Suppliers of Arts and Crafts Materials

Tandy, American Handicraft
Stores in all major cities. See your phone book

Lee Wards
840 N. State Street
Elgin, Illinois 60120

TRIBES:

 1 Ashanti
 2 Baga
 3 Bakota
 4 Bakuba (Bushongo)
 5 Bambara
 6 Bapende
 7 Barotse
 8 Basonge
 9 Baulé
10 Bobo
11 Dan
12 Dogon
13 Ibo
14 Kikuyu
15 Mangbetu
16 Masai
17 N'Debele
18 Nok
19 Nuba
20 Senufo
21 Watusi
22 Yoruba
23 Zulu

Some of the tribes shown on this map no longer exist. Others are found in today's African nations. Country names (in color) were sometimes taken from the predominant tribal group of the area. Key numbers locate only tribes mentioned in this book. There are many others.

The areas of the historic African kingdoms shown on the insert are very approximate. Definite boundaries of ancient kingdoms were not well established. There were many others, such as Zimbabwe, about which very little is known.

HISTORICAL KINGDOMS